T0327978

WELCOME, HOLY SPIRIT

A THEOLOGICAL AND EXPERIENTIAL INTRODUCTION

GORDON T. SMITH

ivp
Academic

An imprint of InterVarsity Press
Downers Grove, Illinois

InterVarsity Press
P.O. Box 1400, Downers Grove, IL 60515-1426
ivpress.com
email@ivpress.com

*InterVarsity Press® is the book-publishing division of InterVarsity Christian Fellowship/USA®,
a movement of students and faculty active on campus at hundreds of universities, colleges,
and schools of nursing in the United States of America, and a member movement of the International
Fellowship of Evangelical Students. For information about local and regional activities, visit intervarsity.org.*

*Scripture quotations, unless otherwise noted, are from the New Revised Standard Version Bible,
copyright © 1989 National Council of the Churches of Christ in the United States of America.
Used by permission. All rights reserved worldwide.*

*The publisher cannot verify the accuracy or functionality of website URLs used in this book beyond
the date of publication.*

Cover design and image composite: David Fassett
Interior design: Daniel van Loon
Images: aqua smoke: © Ablozhka / iStock / Getty Images Plus
flames of fire: © Luis Diaz Devesa / Moment Collection / Getty Images
dove wing: © Siede Preis / DigitalVision / Getty Images
paper background: © Nenov / Moment Collection / Getty Images

ISBN 978-0-8308-5388-5 (print)
ISBN 978-0-8308-5389-2 (digital)

Printed in the United States of America ♾

*InterVarsity Press is committed to ecological stewardship and to the conservation of natural
resources in all our operations. This book was printed using sustainably sourced paper.*

Library of Congress Cataloging-in-Publication Data
Names: Smith, Gordon T., 1953- author.
*Title: Welcome, Holy Spirit : a theological and experiential introduction /
  Gordon T. Smith.*
*Description: Downers Grove, IL : IVP Academic, [2021] | Includes
  bibliographical references and index.*
*Identifiers: LCCN 2021020497 (print) | LCCN 2021020498 (ebook) | ISBN
  9780830853885 (paperback) | ISBN 9780830853892 (ebook)*
*Subjects: LCSH: Holy Spirit. | Holy Spirit—Biblical teaching. |
  Spirituality—Christianity.*
*Classification: LCC BT121.3 .S59 2021 (print) | LCC BT121.3 (ebook) | DDC
  231/.3—dc23*
LC record available at https://lccn.loc.gov/2021020497
LC ebook record available at https://lccn.loc.gov/2021020498

P	25	24	23	22	21	20	19	18	17	16	15	14	13	12	11	10	9	8	7	6	5	4	3	2	1
Y	38	37	36	35	34	33	32	31	30	29	28	27	26	25	24	23	22	21							

for joella

CONTENTS

INTRODUCTION

W HAT DOES IT MEAN TO SAY, in the words of the
Nicene Creed, "I believe in the Holy Spirit"? More specifically, what does it mean to declare all that is included in the affirmation, "I believe in the Holy Spirit, the Lord and Giver of life, who
proceeds from the Father and who with the Father and the Son together is worshiped and glorified, who spoke through the prophets"?[1]

What does it mean to be truly trinitarian—affirming Father,
Son, *and* Spirit—in our faith, worship, Christian life, and witness?
And what does it mean that we believe that the Spirit is the Lord,
the Giver of life?

Answering these questions is not easy; this is complicated territory
that challenges us intellectually and experientially. Thomas Oden has
noted that "no subject of Christian teaching is more prone to fanat-
icism and novelty and subjectivism than the Holy Spirit. . . . The work
of the Spirit deserves especially careful attention precisely because it
is so prone to subjective manipulation and ideological abuse."[2]

---

[1] In the Christian West (in contrast to the Eastern Orthodox Church), it has been the practice
for many centuries to also add "and the Son" (what is typically called the "filioque clause")
so that the creed reads: "who proceeds from the Father and the Son." There might be good
reasons to affirm the distinctive role of the Son in the procession of the Spirit, but given that
it is clearly an addition, our default should be to the original creedal affirmation. I will com-
ment more fully on the dispute in chapter 2.

[2] Thomas Oden, *Life in the Spirit,* Systematic Theology: Volume III (San Francisco: Harper-
San Francisco, 1992), 10.

This is a sobering observation, yet we cannot avoid the question of what it means to believe in the Holy Spirit because it matters too much. There is no other way to live the Christian life except in the fullness of the Spirit. There is no other way to be the church except in the fullness of the Spirit. There is no other way to be the church on mission except in the grace and power of the Spirit. And there is no other way to worship and pray except in the Spirit (Ephesians 6:18). We have so much to gain and nothing to lose by developing the theological and experiential capacity to fully embrace the life and ministry of the Spirit—to be attentive to the presence of the Spirit in the church, in the world, and in our personal life, work, and ministry.

Critical reflection on the person and ministry of the Spirit can be an encouraging and hope-filled exercise, but we need to be discerning. Oden is right; this can go wrong. For our own sake and for the sake of the church and the world, we need to get this right, and this means learning the art of discernment. We need to find the life-giving dynamic captured in 1 Thessalonians 5, when the apostle urges his readers on the one hand to "not quench the Spirit" (v. 19), but then quickly adds: "but test everything" (v. 21). This is our objective: to approach this critical and essential topic with open hearts and eager minds but also with careful thought, willing to ask hard questions that in the end strengthen the life of the church and our own experience of the Holy Spirit. We can turn from both cynicism *and* naiveté; we can be theologically astute *and* eager to live in the grace of the Spirit.

This requires that we ask the right questions—most notably four foundational questions about the Holy Spirit, each of them regarding how the Spirit relates to something else. First and foremost, we ask: What is the relationship between the Spirit and

Christ? As part of that question, we ask what it means to confess the Holy Spirit as one with the Father and the Son within the Holy Trinity.

Second, we ask: What is the relationship between the Spirit and the *created order*? This includes asking about the relationship between the Spirit and the world (the cosmos), and the relationship between the Spirit and materiality—the physicality of the created order.

Third, we ask: What is the relationship between the Spirit and the *Word*—that is, the Scriptures?

And fourth, we ask: What is the relationship between the Spirit and the *church*?

In so many respects, our doctrine of the Holy Spirit—our pneumatology—comes down to these four questions. Thus, for example, if you were to try to get a read on the pneumatology of a particular Christian tradition or denomination, you could ask these four questions. A pneumatology that is faithful to the biblical witness and the creedal heritage of the church will give attention to each of these. All four of them need to arise at some point in our reflections on the person and ministry of the Holy Spirit, but the first is the most critical. Nothing in our understanding of the Spirit is on track if we are not clear about the relationship between the Spirit and Christ. To this end, it is helpful to think of what follows through two images: the compass and the boundary. The compass speaks of the need for clarity about our direction—we need to be clear on our "true north." The boundary—a metaphor from the soccer field—speaks of what it means to be truly "in bounds."

The compass is Christ. Christ Jesus is the north star; he is the author and finisher of our faith. Thus, we keep our eyes on him. Hans Urs von Balthasar expresses this well when he writes: "We must bear in mind . . . that our participation in the Spirit always remains conditioned through the Son sent to us by the Father, the Son of Man who died on the Cross and rose from the realm of the dead and who pours himself out forever to the Church in the Eucharist to prove the Father's love."[3] The first epistle of John stresses that we are not to trust every spirit but test the spirits, and the key evidence is that the spirit that comes from God acknowledges that Jesus Christ has come in the flesh. Thus, the compass for our reflections will be the incarnate, crucified, risen, and ascended Lord. It is not our projections of Christ, but the Christ who is the embodied, suffering, and ascended Lamb.

This point cannot be overstated. Many Christian communities have what would seem to be a powerful emphasis on the ministry of the Spirit and insist that they are "Christ-centered." Yet frequently the Christ of whom they speak is a "spiritized" Christ— not the incarnate, crucified, and ascended Lord. Thus, we must insist that the reference point for the ministry of the Spirit is the Christ who is revealed in the Scriptures.

If the compass is Christ, the boundaries of the playing field are what we mean to speak of God as both one and triune. We need to stay within the ancient creedal witness to the triunity of God, and also need to consider some of the ancient trinitarian heresies and note how remarkably relevant they are today.

If we stay within these historic boundaries and keep our focus on Christ, we can eagerly delve into these reflections with an open heart and an eager mind, ever open to new and surprising

---

[3]Hans Urs von Balthasar, *Spirit and Institution,* Explorations in Theology IV, trans. Edward T. Oakes (San Francisco: Ignatius Press, 1995), 343-44.

expressions of the Spirit in our world, in our churches, and in our individual lives. We will study what it means to believe in the Spirit while we pray: "Come, Holy Spirit, come."

In our learning, one of the wisest things we can do is read widely and be open to the witness of other theological and spiritual traditions than our own. Frequently, it seems that Christians only read books or listen to speakers on the Holy Spirit to affirm their own perspective or experience. But we need the gentle corrective and wisdom of others. Thus, in what follows I will not hesitate to draw on Catholic, Orthodox, evangelical, and Pentecostal voices, along with other perspectives, including those of the Global South. Catholics need to be reading Pentecostal theologians and writers; evangelicals have much to learn from Orthodox voices.

Further, we need to consider the ways in which the church traditions where we were formed—as children or through our initiation into Christian faith—understood and engaged the Spirit. We need to come to terms with both the strengths and the limitations of our own theological and spiritual traditions/experience.

So as you read, keep three perspectives in mind. First, think in terms of your own denomination. Our experience of the Spirit is never purely personal or individual; our encounter with the grace of God is always derivative of the life and witness of the faith community. Thus, it is appropriate to ask: What is the theology and experience of the Spirit in the church community that has formed you and of which you are a part?

Second, ask about your own experience. What does all of this talk about the Holy Spirit mean for your own journey of faith in Christ? Where are you being nudged, called, or beckoned? What is being asked of you, and in what ways might it be that the Spirit could be invited to be more fully present in your life experience—in your relationship with Christ, with the church, and in other relationships? Look back as well and allow your own experience of the grace of the Spirit to inform your reading and reflection on this crucial topic.

And third, ask this question: How does your learning about the person and ministry of the Holy Spirit inform your engagement with the world—with your neighbors, with those of other religious faiths, and with your social and cultural context? What does your learning about the Spirit mean for your personal engagement with what God is doing in the world? What does it mean for your work and for living out your vocation?

As I have noted, in order to say "I believe in the Holy Spirit" we need to have clarity about the relationship between the Holy Spirit and Christ Jesus. Thus, the first two foundational chapters will probe this relationship by considering the Holy Spirit in Luke and Acts and then the witness to the Holy Spirit in the Gospel of John. Then I will address the other questions: The Spirit and creation, the Spirit and the Word and the Spirit and the church. And, in between, attention will be given to the Spirit and personal experience. But first, a prelude: an invitation to consider the classic metaphors of the Spirit that emerge in Scripture and that are testified to in the history of the church.

IMAGES AND METAPHORS FOR THE HOLY SPIRIT

O NE OF THE KEY DEVELOPMENTS in Christian theology and hermeneutics in the last generation has been a rethinking of the place of metaphor in language, communication, and understanding, and thus in our response to what we come to see to be true or significant—and, in particular, in how we speak about God.[1] We have come to see that we cannot read Scripture well without having some sense of how metaphors function in language and thought: that, indeed, we cannot think theologically without the use of metaphor. This means we should be students of metaphors and realize how powerful they are in shaping our understanding and experience.

We might ask, then, how metaphor and images of the Holy Spirit in Scripture might inform our understanding and experience of the grace of the Holy Spirit and also serve as a teaching tool. There are five key metaphors for the Holy Spirit used in Scripture: the wind or breath of God, the oil of anointing, the

---

[1]Perhaps as influential as any theologian in this regard is Sallie McFague, who suggests that metaphor is the only way we can engage the mystery of God. See, in particular, *Metaphorical Theology: Models of God in Religious Language* (Philadelphia: Fortress Press, 1982). Some have challenged McFague, suggesting that she goes beyond the bounds of the biblical witness in her use of metaphors for God. Regardless, her main point remains: to speak of God we must use metaphor.

flame of God, living or flowing water, and the dove or the hovering bird. Is there an image that is particularly meaningful to you—and, perhaps, is most present to you now—that evokes for you the gracious ministry, presence, and grace of the Holy Spirit? Further, is there an image that might be particularly meaningful for the church community of which you are a part, given that that image is evocative within your cultural and social context?

In what follows, I am going to highlight these five key metaphors for the Holy Spirit in Scripture. These metaphors are lenses into the mystery of the Holy Spirit, and yet they have limits. We must not overplay these metaphors or read more into them than the biblical witness justifies. We can learn to accept the *limits* of metaphor so they are not misused. We cannot arbitrarily determine meaning by saying, "Well, this image means this to *me*." We need to let text and context shape our appreciation for an image, along with the witness of key voices in the history of the church. Further, the metaphors do not have a one-to-one correlation to what they are depicting. It is not that the meaning is ambiguous; rather, the image is multitextured. That is why with the Holy Spirit we rightly speak of multiple metaphors or word pictures, and see how they complement and reinforce one another.

With these caveats, we can now consider the five key or central metaphors for the Holy Spirit in Scripture and allow them to shape our understanding and experience.

THE SPIRIT AS THE WIND OR BREATH OF GOD

For many biblical scholars, this is the primary image of the Spirit in the Scriptures. It certainly seems to be the most common. However, as Anthony Thiselton notes, it is not always clear when the Hebrew *ruach* (which can denote "wind," "breath," or "spirit") is speaking of breath or wind, or when it does actually indicate the third person of the Trinity.[2] Yet there are uses of *ruach* that are indisputably a reference to the Spirit, and these merit our attention. Each is significant to our understanding of and appreciation for the ministry of the Spirit in the world, in the church, and in our own lives.

The biblical narrative opens with a description of the breath of God that brings order and beauty out of darkness and chaos: "In the beginning when God created the heavens and the earth, the earth was a formless void and darkness covered the face of the deep, while a wind from God swept over the face of the waters" (Genesis 1:1-2). From this grand opening, we come to the creation of human persons in Genesis 2:7: "Then the LORD God formed man from the dust of the ground, and breathed into his nostrils the breath of life; and the man became a living being." Taken together, these remarkable texts give us an appreciation for the physicality of the created order as good but not truly alive until it is infused with the breath of God, the Spirit who animates all of creation.

The Spirit inspires—that is, in-breathes—and what receives this breath comes alive. The Scriptures are inspired or in-breathed by the Spirit, and it is this inspiration that makes the Scriptures a life-giving text (more on this in chapter 6). The created order and the Scriptures are alive—living—by virtue of the *wind* of God.

Connected with this is the vision of the prophet Ezekiel, who wrote to the people of Judah while they were in exile. Ezekiel's own sense of call came through the breath of God—on the wind, one

---

[2] Anthony C. Thistleton, *A Shorter Guide to the Spirit: Bible, Doctrine, Experience* (Grand Rapids, MI: Eerdmans, 2016), 10-11.

might say (Ezekiel 1:4). But not only did his calling to prophetic ministry come on the wind, but also his vision of death and life in Ezekiel 37, one of the most evocative examples of this metaphor in Scripture. He observes the unforgettable valley of dead bones and is himself taken up in the new life that is being breathed into those bones:

> Then he said to me, "Prophesy to the breath, prophesy, mortal, and say to the breath: Thus says the Lord GOD: Come from the four winds, O breath, and breathe upon these slain, that they may live." I prophesied as he commanded me, and the breath came into them, and they lived, and stood on their feet, a vast multitude.
>
> Then he said to me, "Mortal, these bones are the whole house of Israel. They say, 'Our bones are dried up, and our hope is lost; we are cut off completely.' Therefore prophesy, and say to them, Thus says the Lord GOD: I am going to open your graves, and bring you up from your graves, O my people; and I will bring you back to the land of Israel. And you shall know that I am the LORD, when I open your graves, and bring you up from your graves, O my people. I will put my spirit within you, and you shall live, and I will place you on your own soil; then you shall know that I, the LORD, have spoken and will act, says the LORD." (Ezekiel 37:9-14)

Later, Pentecost is described through the lens of this metaphor: "When the day of Pentecost had come, they were all together in one place. And suddenly from heaven there came a sound like the rush of a violent wind, and it filled the entire house where they were sitting" (Acts 2:1-2). We come to Pentecost aware of the teaching of Jesus, where the image of the Spirit as breath or wind is quite prominent. First, in John 3:8 Jesus speaks of the presence and grace of the Spirit at Christian initiation, saying that we must be born from above, born of the Spirit. Then he adds that the wind blows where the wind blows, clearly indicating that this initiation into Christian faith is not something that we as individuals or as the church control. It is of God, more specifically of the Spirit. Second, we have the remarkable conclusion to the Gospel of John, when Jesus breathes on his disciples and exhorts them to "receive the Holy Spirit" (John 20:22).

It is appropriate to read these references in light of Genesis and Ezekiel and affirm that the animating and inspiriting grace of the Spirit is at the heart of creation, at the heart of the church and thus at the heart of life of the Christian. The same one who "himself gives to all mortals life and breath and all things" (Acts 17:25) is the one who infuses *our* broken lives and communities with new and healing life through his breath, the *wind* of God. And so our yearning for life is then a yearning to be filled with the Spirit so that, in the language of Ezekiel, we might live.

THE SPIRIT AS THE OIL OF ANOINTING

The metaphor of oil is a powerful way by which the grace of the Holy Spirit is appropriated into the life and witness of the Christian community. Typically, those churches that take the ministry of the Spirit seriously will be ever ready with the oil of anointing to represent the presence and power of the Spirit in their community life and in the life of each individual Christian believer. This image is definitely linked to the ministry of the church, and will typically thus be connected to the laying on of hands in Christian community. We are not self-anointed; we are anointed by those who represent Christ to us through the church.

The image of oil in the New Testament is an echo of what we find in the Old Testament. Exodus 25:6, Leviticus 8:30, and

Numbers 4:16 all speak of the holiness of the oil of anointing that sets apart someone or something for a particular purpose for the people of God. Exodus 30:30 reads: "You shall anoint Aaron and his sons, and consecrate them, in order that they may serve me as priests." Note also the reference to anointing in 1 Samuel 16:13 and the anointing of David by Samuel.

In the New Testament we find that Jesus, in continuity with both the prophetic and priestly lines, is anointed as Messiah and prophet, and is conscious that in this anointing the Spirit of God rests on him and has set him aside for the work to which he has been called. At the beginning of his ministry—described in Luke 4—he references the words of the prophet Isaiah in speaking about his own call and anointing:

> The spirit of the Lord GOD is upon me,
>   because the LORD has anointed me;
> he has sent me to bring good news to the oppressed,
>   to bind up the brokenhearted,
> to proclaim liberty to the captives,
>   and release to the prisoners. (Isaiah 61:1)

The early church testified to this in Acts 10:38, when Peter speaks of Jesus as one who was *anointed* with the Holy Spirit and with power.

Many have also been intrigued by the references in both Luke and John to the women who anointed the feet of Jesus. In the Gospel of John it is Mary, the sister of Martha and Lazarus, who anoints Jesus' feet (John 12:1-8). But in Luke the woman is unnamed and referenced as one who is a "sinner" (Luke 7:38-50). What are the Gospel writers telling us here? What does it mean that someone from the margins, one might say, provided this anointing—not on the head, the typical place of anointing (as

Jesus himself notes in verse 46), but the feet? Is there some sense that this from-the-margins anointing was a further sign of Jesus' identity and calling?

The precedent of anointing for those in leadership—as priests, prophets, or kings—in the history of Israel and then in Jesus has found expression in the church in the setting aside of those who are called into religious leadership. Those ordained to preach and preside within the Christian community are confirmed for this ministry through having hands laid on them and being anointed with oil. The oil represents the presence and power of the Spirit on the life and ministry of those ordained: we lay hands on them, we anoint them with oil, and we pray that the Spirit who has called them to this ministry would empower them and guide them in this work. Again, this is not a self-anointing but the confirmation of the Christian community that this individual has been called of the Spirit and has chosen to accept this call and depend on the Spirit's gifting and empowerment to serve with humility as the representative of Christ in the midst of God's people.

And yet the New Testament also seems to speak of the anointing of all of God's people. In 1 John 2:20 and 27 the writer of the epistle speaks of each of his readers as having received the anointing grace of God. Then also 2 Corinthians 1:21-22 reads: "But it is God who establishes us with you in Christ and has anointed us, by putting his seal on us and giving us his Spirit in our hearts as a first installment."

It is no surprise, then, that the early church eagerly embraced oil as the symbol of the presence of the Spirit at Christian initiation —ideally linked to water baptism. There is a deep logic here. In Christian initiation, why would we not follow the precedent of Acts 8:14-18, or that of the experience of Paul when Ananias came to him and laid hands on him that he would receive the gift of the Spirit (Acts 9:17)? And the most compelling symbol to represent this gift is oil. Thus for the ancient church, Christian initiation was a twofold rite: water baptism and the laying on of hands, with the oil of anointing to speak to the grace and presence of the Spirit in the life of the new believer. The church, through a presiding minister, anoints the now-baptized Christian, inviting the Spirit to rest on, guide, and empower this new follower of Christ.

There is another distinct usage of the oil of anointing: the ministry the church has to those who are sick, both physically and emotionally. Perhaps following the precedent set by Jesus' disciples—see Mark 6:13, where the disciples were praying for and anointing the sick—we have the clear call in James that those who are sick are invited to approach the elders so that they can be prayed for with the laying on of hands and anointed with oil (James 5:14). While there is not in this text an explicit link to the Holy Spirit, we can take it as such because the readers of James would have assumed a link between oil and the Spirit. Thus, Christian communities with a more explicit understanding of the ministry of the Spirit typically see the anointing of the sick as a prayer for the Spirit to come and bring healing and strength to those who are in pain and suffering.

In each of these, the typical practice in the history of the church has been for the person presiding, whether priest or pastor or elder, to make the sign of the cross on the forehead. But for some, much more oil is used. In some cases, the rite of initiation includes water baptism and the laying on of hands, with the head of the newly baptized literally bathed with oil.

Finally, we must note the link between oil and joy, reflecting Hebrews 1:9, where it is said that Jesus received the "oil of gladness."

Ambrose of Milan made this an important theme in his "On the Holy Spirit." He quotes Hebrews and insists that the Holy Spirit in Christ is the oil of gladness that, as he puts it, is "the joining together of many graces giving a sweet fragrance."[3] Ambrose goes to some length to demonstrate that the references to oil in the life and ministry of Jesus are references to the Holy Spirit.

But what most catches attention in Ambrose's references to oil and the Holy Spirit is how he links oil and joy—saying that, indeed, those who have been anointed by the Spirit are graced with a profound and resilient gladness. Those who serve the church in the fullness of the Spirit do so with joy. Those who are initiated into the faith enter into a community that is marked by a deep and resilient joy (see Acts 2:46). We can also affirm that those who are anointed as the sick and suffering come to know the grace of God—evident in the joy that comes in healing but also in the grace of God in the midst of suffering when healing is delayed.

THE SPIRIT AS FIRE

In his little book *The Divine Conquest*, A. W. Tozer devotes a whole chapter to the image of the Holy Spirit as fire.[4] Tozer was taken by the idea that fire indicated the presence of God: whether it was Moses at the burning bush that was not consumed (Exodus 3:2); the fire at the center of Israel's wilderness camp and then in the holy of holies; or the experience of Ezekiel, for whom fire is linked to splendor and the glory of God (Ezekiel 1:4, 27-28).[5] Then, of

---

[3] Ambrose of Milan, "Three Books of St. Ambrose on the Holy Spirit," in *St. Ambrose: Select Works and Letters*, ed. Philip Schaff and Henry Wace, vol. 10, A Select Library of the Nicene and Post-Nicene Fathers of the Christian Church, Second Series (New York: Christian Literature Company, 1896), 107 (1.9.94).

[4] A. W. Tozer, *The Divine Conquest* (Harrisburg, PA: Christian Publications, 1950). See chapter VIII, 94-109.

[5] Tozer, *Divine Conquest*, 97.

course, fire is also referenced at Pentecost alongside the mighty wind. There is something powerful in the idea that the "appearance of fire" over the tabernacle for the people of Israel in the wilderness now speaks of the Spirit who at Pentecost was poured out over all people and all of creation.

As Tozer observes, fire indicating the presence of God is a key theme in Scripture. We read that John the Baptist foretold that one was coming, more powerful than he, who would baptize with the Holy Spirit and *fire* (Matthew 3:11). And, indeed, on the day of Pentecost, what appeared over the disciples in the midst of the wind were divided tongues of fire (Acts 2:2-3). Tozer concludes that the reference in Matthew to baptism with the Holy Spirit and fire is a sobering one—the text speaks of chaff that will be burned up with unquenchable fire (Matthew 3:12).[6] This fire does not destroy but brings healing and wholeness. It is a purgation that may not be all that comfortable but is deeply needed. This is a reminder that we need to get beyond the idea that the presence of God is all about nice or powerful feelings—the not-uncommon notion that the manifest presence of God is about ecstasy and heightened emotion. Rather, this image reminds us that those who truly long for the presence of God are willing to go through pain and discomfort akin to the rehabilitation program for the addict that leads to resolution, healing, and wholeness.

No one in the history of the church has spoken to this more powerfully than the sixteenth-century Spanish mystic and reformer Saint John of the Cross. His extended poem "The Living Flame of God," along with his own commentary on the poem, speaks of the Spirit as the fire that purifies: the fire of God that

---

[6]Tozer, *Divine Conquest,* 100.

courses through our beings and orders our affections. This is the image for those who, like the addict, long for freedom and crave holiness deep in their souls. They are willing to face purgation in order to know healing. The image is not so much that of a flame that is alive as it is a flame that "makes the soul alive in the living God."[7]

What is striking in this poem is that the presence and power of the Spirit as a flame is the fruit of love.[8] The love of God is poured into our hearts by the Holy Spirit (Romans 5:5), and this love longs for us to be made whole. This makes us not comfortable but free; we become those who lean into the love of God, knowing that the Spirit's grace and power, over the long haul, will lead us to holiness. In other words, the Spirit does not intend to make us feel good. Rather, the Spirit, the living flame of love, *purifies*. As John of the Cross notes, we might sometimes feel the warmth of this love, but he stresses that it "is not gentle, but afflictive."[9] The essential emotional quality to this transformative work of the Spirit is "dry." He references Lamentations and the fire in the bones that instructs us, and then also Psalm 66:10-12, which speaks of being tried by fire.[10]

This image, then, calls us to reverence and awe. It reminds us that we are in the presence of the God who is a "consuming fire" (Hebrews 12:29). Thus, no doubt our liturgies and approaches to

---

[7]John of the Cross, *The Collected Works of St. John of the Cross*, trans. Kieran Kavanaugh and Otilio Rodriguez (Washington, DC: ICS Publications, 1979), 581.

[8]By this logic, Clark Pinnock would title his theology of the Holy Spirit *Flame of Love* (Downers Grove, IL: InterVarsity Press, 1999).

[9]John of the Cross, *Collected Works*, 586. These are hard words for those who want comfort and ease, especially when John insists that "neither is the flame refreshing and peaceful, but it is consuming and contentious" (586). This is short-term pain for the sake of long-term gain; we want freedom from our disordered desires. We want to grow up and not remain as coddled infants.

[10]John of the Cross, *Collected Works*, 587.

worship will be marked by delight and joy, but just as surely we will want to bend the knee, to be silent in the presence of the holy one of Israel, and to graciously if not eagerly accept the penitential way. This image of the Spirit is a fitting one for the season of Lent, as we pray that the Holy Spirit will come and burn through our sin-sick souls and make us whole.

If images of the Holy Spirit have particular resonance with an ethnic group or culture, holy fire comes to mind when we think of the people and land of Azerbaijan. The name of the country means "the place of sacred fire," and in the south, near the city of Astara, there is a remarkable blending of water and fire at a spring known as Yanar Bulag. Continually lit by natural gas, it is known to those who head there on pilgrimage as the "fire spring." Further north is the fifth-century Armenian Orthodox community of Nij, in what is the ancient region of Caucasian Albania. The church there has on its wall a fascinating depiction of flames coming out of three strands of the cross. One cannot help but wonder, given the significance of a living flame to these ancient people, if this would not be the image of the Spirit that would most resonate with them.

Finally, this image of the Holy Spirit is also associated with calling or vocation. The burning bush for Moses was the occasion of his calling to partner with God in leading the people of Israel out of Egypt, and it is interesting to see an allusion to fire in Paul's exhortation to Timothy: "For this reason I remind you to rekindle the gift of God that is within you through the laying on of my hands; for God did not give us a spirit of cowardice, but rather a spirit of power and of love and of self-discipline" (2 Timothy 1:6-7).

The reference to "rekindling" or, as in other translations, "fan into flame," is linked to what follows: that this gift, this flame, indicates not the Spirit of fear or cowardice, but rather of power, love, and discipline. Thus, it seems that the two potential meanings come together here—the idea of calling, but also of how we are called to live out our calling with depth and maturity and a life of holiness, a theme that is emphasized throughout 2 Timothy. We see this link as well in Isaiah 6. The evocative question, "Whom shall I send, and who will go for us?" (verse 8) is preceded by the living coal that is taken from the altar and touches the lips of the prophet (verse 6), removing his guilt so that, with clarity and con-viction, he can respond to the call with the words, "Here am I; send me!" (verse 8).

THE SPIRIT AS LIVING WATER

There are hints along the way in the biblical narrative that may suggest linking the Holy Spirit with water, but it is without doubt Jesus himself, in the Gospel of John, who speaks this way about the presence and ministry of the Spirit. In John 4, he is at the well with the woman of Samaria and in his theological conversation with her he speaks of the water from the well but then also of the *living* water and then concludes: "The water that I will give will become [for those who drink of it] a spring of water gushing up to eternal life" (John 4:14). We might wonder, as we read of this noon-time encounter between this woman and Jesus what is meant by this water—that is, what is this living water to which Jesus refers? But then a few chapters later we are left with no doubt whatsoever as John makes the link oh-so-clear:

> On the last day of the festival, the great day, while Jesus was standing there, he cried out, "Let anyone who is thirsty come to me, and let the one who believes in me drink. As the scripture has said, 'Out of the believer's heart shall flow rivers of living water.'"

Now he said this about the Spirit, which believers in him were to receive; for as yet there was no Spirit, because Jesus was not yet glorified. (John 7:37-39)

While there is no question that there is something of comfort and encouragement in the image of still water, when this image is linked to the Spirit the usual referent is to living or flowing water, as for example we see it and hear it in the words of the prophet Isaiah: "For I will pour out water on the thirsty land, and streams on the dry ground; I will pour out my spirit on your descendants, and my blessing on your offspring" (Isaiah 44:3).

In Ezekiel, the prophet links the promise that God will "sprinkle clean water upon you" and "I will remove from your body the heart of stone and give you a heart of flesh" with "I will put my spirit within you" (Ezekiel 36:25-27) all on the assumption that the people would be cleansed and made new. And in Joel, the reference that is then picked up by Peter on the day of Pentecost, the Spirit is "poured out" on all flesh (Joel 2:28-29). Further, it is alluded to by the apostle Paul when he speaks of the one Spirit of whom we drink (1 Corinthians 12:13).

As noted earlier, the image of the Spirit as a living flame would seem to resonate deeply with the people of central Asia. Similarly, living water is a profoundly important image in both ancient Chinese and Japanese culture and religion. Chinese philosophical writings often make the assumption that the highest good and the highest form of excellence is found in the pursuit of water. And it is always the case that if you were to visit a classic Japanese garden, there will be a strategically placed fountain or stream and, as you wander through the garden, you will more than likely more than once hear the gentle sound of flowing water—gentle, not cascading, tumbling over a rock or through a bamboo pipe—*flowing* in that this is not still or stagnant water, but water that is present to us as something that is alive. And thus we might ask: What does it mean to announce to those of East Asian descent that if they are longing for living water, much like the Samaritan woman, they will find that living water by coming to Jesus?

If this is the case, I cannot help but wonder if this image should be front and center for those who minister in and for the church in East Asia or among the diaspora. And more, that for whoever it is that we are called to serve, that we be attentive to which of these images might be most evocative and meaningful to *these* people, whoever they are, in this context and with these cultural sensitivities.

For those of us for whom in walking the shore we find deep comfort in the sound of the surf breaking gently on the beach or, indeed, that we know what it means to have a sense of deep clarity and comfort that comes in the intentional wander through a Japanese garden, there is little doubt that this image captures for us a deep yearning for life. The Samaritan woman was still likely a little confused when she pled with Jesus to "give me this water, so that I may never be thirsty," but we get it: this is the living water without which we cannot live; this is the living water and so with open hands and open hearts we ask that this water, this Spirit, would be poured into our tepid, thirsty souls.

The Spirit as Dove

Finally, we come to the image of the Spirit as portrayed to us as a hovering bird or the dove who descends from heaven. This image can be addressed more briefly, since the meaning is quite straightforward.

All four Gospel narratives refer to the appearance of a dove coming on Jesus at his baptism by John at the Jordan River (Matthew 3:16; Mark 1:10; Luke 3:22; John 1:32). In Luke, for example, we read that "the Holy Spirit descended upon him in bodily form like a dove." The image of the hovering dove evokes an appreciation of the Spirit as the one who leans over and into the created order—present to all of God's creation as the source of grace, comfort, encouragement, and guidance.[11] The primary referent for the image of the dove is surely the diverse ways in which the Spirit was present to Jesus—leading him into the desert and guiding his steps and his teaching. Indeed, as Jesus himself acknowledged when he rose to speak in the synagogue, quoting Isaiah about himself, "the Spirit of the Lord is upon me" (Luke 4:18).

In the history of the church, the Christian leader who is perhaps most associated with this image is Gregory the Great, who was pope AD 590–604. Gregory is typically depicted with a dove on his shoulder, representing the guidance of the Holy Spirit in his life, and particularly in his speaking and teaching. The legend goes that his servant saw a dove hovering near him when he was working on sermons on the prophet Ezekiel, and Gregory was seemingly attending to this dove as he wrote. Gregory was a significant missionary leader; he was the one who commissioned the Augustine who became Augustine of Canterbury to take the gospel to the British Isles. He also had a profound impact on liturgy and worship,

---

[11]Some might be inclined to link the dove who descends on Jesus with the reference in Genesis to a dove that returned to Noah's ark with an olive branch—and thus make a link between the dove as an image of peace and Jesus as the Prince of Peace. But this is not a link made in the New Testament, and thus it might be pressing things too far to make this association. And we do not need to; each image is rich enough without trying to press more into it than is intended by the biblical text.

notably through the musical style known as the Gregorian chant, which dominated Christian worship for centuries.

Perhaps it is because of the influence of this extraordinary church leader that the image of the dove, more than that of any of the others, speaks of the ministry of the Holy Spirit as guide and encourager. This is the image we are drawn to when we long for the confidence that the Spirit is hovering over us and, as with Gregory, present to us through wise counsel in our speaking and acting. Preachers, teachers, knowledge leaders, and organizational decision makers long to know the assuring and subtle but sure witness of the Spirit to heart and mind. We are eager to know that the Spirit is present to us in the challenges, setbacks, and opportunities we face, whether at home or in the marketplace. We long to be guided by the Spirit.

Thus we may pray, using this image: come heavenly dove, grant us wisdom, grant us clarity, grant us discernment so that as we speak and act we have the courage to say what needs to be said and do what needs to be done. There is no doubt that we do not always get this right; we must eschew any presumption that we always hear the Spirit correctly. We need to learn discernment. We need to remember that we are easily self-deceived, and that we all have the potential for rationalizations. That is why this image alone may not be enough to draw us into the grace of the Spirit; we need the other images as correctives to any inclination we might have to equate our thoughts with the thoughts of the Spirit.

• • •

Notice that all five images suggest movement, and thus life: a living flame, wind or the breath of God, running water, the anointing oil, and the hovering dove. The Spirit of God is not static. Further, each of these images may seem to be impersonal, and thus the point must be made that the Spirit is indeed a person. Yet the metaphors are indispensable to our understanding and experience of the Holy Spirit. Ancient and contemporary poetry, hymnody, and spiritual song have captured one or more of these images, and especially the prayer "Come, Holy Spirit" provides images that call forth our deep longing to be a people who live in the grace and power of the Spirit. "Come Holy Ghost, Our Hearts Inspire" by Charles Wesley, one of the greatest hymn writers in the history of the church, draws on three of the images:

> Come, Holy Ghost, our hearts inspire,
>   Let us Thy influence prove;
> Source of the old prophetic fire,
>   Fountain of light and love.
> Come, Holy Ghost, (for moved by Thee,
>   Thy prophets wrote and spoke,)
> Unlock the truth, Thyself the Key,
>   Unseal the Sacred Book.
> Expand Thy wings, prolific Dove,
>   Brood o'er our nature's night;
> On our disorder'd spirits move,
>   And let there now be light.
> God through Himself we then shall know
>   If Thou *within us* shine;
> And sound, with all Thy saints below,
>   The depths of love Divine.[12]

---

[12]John Wesley and Charles Wesley, *The Poetical Works of John and Charles Wesley*, ed. G. Osborn, vol. 1 (London: Wesleyan-Methodist Conference Office, 1868), 238-39.

In our worship, we can be alert to when these metaphors emerge through the pen of hymn and song writers. We can consciously attend to the Spirit in our singing by appreciating how the metaphor is a window into the work of the Spirit in our lives, in the church, and in the world.

CHAPTER ONE

THE SPIRIT IN THE GOSPEL OF LUKE AND ACTS

The Ascension and Pentecost

O NE OF THE MOST HELPFUL WAYS to enter into reflections on the ministry of the Holy Spirit is through considering the counterpoint between the *ascension* of the risen Christ and the gift of the Spirit on *Pentecost*, ten days later. It is clear from Scripture that these two events need to be understood in the light of the other. Neither stands alone.

Of course, all the great christological events matter: incarnation, cross, resurrection, and then, following the ascension and Pentecost, the consummation of the reign of Christ at the fulfillment of history. Thus Pentecost can only be understood in light of the incarnation and the cross, and it only makes sense when we view it as the inauguration of a new dispensation of the Spirit that anticipates what is witnessed to in the book of Revelation.

Yet it is helpful to give *particular* attention to the interplay between the ascension and the gift of the Spirit at Pentecost, to see these events as pivotal to the experience and witness of the church—and more, as central and pivotal *together*. They are distinct but inseparable in our understanding of redemptive history and what it means for the church to be the church.

In particular, we must consider this interconnection between the ascension and Pentecost through the two New Testament books penned by Luke: the witness to Jesus as recorded in the Gospel of Luke, and then the book of Acts where we have the story of the early church. In Luke, the Spirit and Jesus. In Acts, the Spirit and the church. Part I of this narrative is the story of Jesus and the Spirit, leading to the ascension as the grand finale with Jesus' words that anticipate Pentecost. Part II is the story of the church and the Spirit, beginning with the ascension and Pentecost. In the Jesus story, we recognize that we can only appreciate Jesus in light of the presence and anointing power of the Spirit. Then we see that, in like fashion, the early church only makes sense when we see it in light of the presence and power of the Spirit. The inflection point between them, at the end of the Gospel of Luke and the opening of the book of Acts, is the ascension and Pentecost.

JESUS AND THE SPIRIT

The Gospel of Luke is a powerful depiction of how, from the incarnation, to Jesus' life and ministry, to the cross and the resurrection, leading up to the ascension, the Spirit is empowering, guiding, and witnessing to the inner life of Jesus. The Jesus story makes no sense apart from the remarkable work of the Spirit.

Before Jesus, the story begins with a group of fascinating characters: Zechariah and Elizabeth and their son, John, and Mary the mother of Jesus. Luke speaks of all four of them in the light of the Spirit's presence and power in their lives and their words.

First, Zechariah is told by the angel Gabriel that his wife, Elizabeth, would bear a son to be named John—whom we would come to know as John the Baptist—and that his son "will be filled with the Holy Spirit" (Luke 1:15). Then Gabriel comes to Mary and announces that "the Holy Spirit will come upon you, and the power of the Most High will overshadow you," and that the one to be born of her womb will be called the Son of God (Luke 1:35). Mary accepts this word and then heads to the hill country to the house of Elizabeth, her cousin. When they meet, Luke makes it a point to record that Elizabeth "was filled with the Holy Spirit" and proclaimed to the young Mary: "Blessed are you among women, and blessed is the fruit of your womb" (Luke 1:41-42). Mary's response is the extraordinary words that we know as the "Magnificat"—her testimony to her Son, whom she magnifies, and who will fulfill the promise of God to Abraham (Luke 1:55). The Magnificat is followed by the prophecy of Zechariah, who "was filled with the Holy Spirit" (Luke 1:67), and spoke of the role of his son, John, who would prepare the way for the son of Mary.

Yet another noteworthy player in the arrival of the Christ-child is a man in Jerusalem named Simeon, about whom Luke writes that "the Holy Spirit rested on him" (Luke 2:25). He was guided by the Spirit to the temple on the day that Mary and Joseph brought the baby Jesus there for the customary dedication rites. Simeon is a classic example of what we mean when we say that the Spirit's role is to lead us to Christ.

What is impressive in this account is the constant reference to the witness and filling of the Spirit. The Spirit makes it all happen. The human players matter; Mary, for example, must say the words "let it be with me according to your word" (Luke 1:38). But it is all in response to the anointing and empowerment of the Spirit. These references help us to see that the Spirit is not merely a by-product of the coming of the Messiah. As we will see in a coming chapter, the Spirit is active in creation and history from the beginning. And here, the Gospel writer highlights how the Spirit is present and active in the life and ministry of Jesus from the beginning.

Jesus emerges on the scene when John the Baptist was preaching and baptizing. Jesus was also baptized, and we read that while he was praying, "the heaven was opened, and the Holy Spirit descended upon him in bodily form like a dove" (Luke 3:21-22). This coincided with the voice that also came from heaven, "You are my Son, the Beloved" (Luke 3:22). Father, Son, and Holy Spirit came together, with the Spirit coming upon Jesus and thereby launching his earthly ministry.

As noted in the prelude, the image of the dove is compelling and evocative. In this context, it likely speaks to the idea of a *personal* presence—a hovering and guiding presence—that superintends and guides Jesus. In his ministry, Jesus is dependent on the Spirit and teaches in the fullness of the Spirit. Specifically, the Spirit is "upon him." The Spirit who came upon Jesus in the form of a dove at his baptism was present at his conception and superintended the events around Jesus' birth. Then, as Jesus moves into his ministry, Jesus is led by the Spirit, anointed by the Spirit, and empowered by the Spirit. In all of this, Jesus knows the joy that is the fruit of the Spirit's presence and power in his life and ministry. Indeed, we read that Jesus rejoices "in the Spirit" (Luke 10:21).

Then, Jesus anticipates that this same Spirit will be present to his disciples *in like manner*. Before Jesus arrives and is baptized by John the Baptist, John speaks of how Jesus "will baptize you with the Holy Spirit and fire" (Luke 3:16). Later in the Gospel of Luke, Jesus is speaking and assures his hearers that "the heavenly Father [will] give the Holy Spirit to those who ask him" (Luke 11:13). The suggestion would seem to be—and we will come back to this—that the gift is given but that it requires intentionality and receptiveness on the part of the disciples.

At the end of the Gospel of Luke, Jesus tells his disciples that they are to wait in Jerusalem until they receive the gift, which he speaks of as "power from on high" (Luke 24:49). The same Spirit that was with him will now, in like fashion, be with them.

THE SPIRIT AND THE EARLY CHURCH

Part II takes us to the book of Acts, where Luke describes the relationship between the Spirit and the church. Here we have what almost seems like an echo of what we have just witnessed regarding the Spirit and Jesus. There is no reason to force this into a one-to-one parallel—Jesus and the Spirit, and then the church and the Spirit—yet the themes that emerge in the book of Acts certainly reflect what seems to be a counterpart to the experience of Jesus witnessed to in the Gospel of Luke.

The first thing to note is the reference to the *reception* of the Spirit, at Pentecost and then throughout the book of Acts. On Pentecost, Peter's response to those who heard his proclamation was that they should repent and be baptized for the forgiveness of their sins and thereby would receive the gift of the Holy Spirit (Acts 2:38). It is no surprise, then, that Paul's conversion includes Ananias coming to Paul with a definite intent: that his sight would be restored, but also that he would "be filled with the Holy Spirit" (Acts 9:17). This is a theme in Acts: that those who come to faith in Christ know the gift of the Spirit and are able to witness to it. Sometimes, the gift is given without intentionality, such as when Cornelius and his household experience their own Pentecost. But more common is what we see when Peter and John went to Samaria and "prayed for them that they might receive the Holy Spirit" (Acts 8:15).

From the expectation that the Spirit would be given at Christian initiation in Acts 2:38 to the practice of the laying on of hands with the explicit request for the Spirit, we can conclude two things. First, the gift of the Spirit is a birthright—an integral dimension of what it means to come to faith in Christ. And second, it would seem appropriate to formalize the laying on of hands with the invitation, "Come, Holy Spirit, come." I will speak more to this when we come to chapter 4. The point here is that, just as the initiation of both the life and ministry of Jesus must be attributed to the Spirit, the inception of the church is a Spirit-infused event.

Second, the book of Acts is the story the Spirit creating the church; the church was the fruit of divine empowerment. The beginning of the church could not be explained other than by saying that God had chosen to act in Christ and by the Spirit to bring about a community of faith, learning, and witness that was marked by an awareness of the transforming grace of God in both word and deed.

The early church was receptive, recognized the primacy of the Spirit, and was responsive to the immediate witness of the Spirit. What is described in the book of Acts is not so much a church doing strategic planning as a community that was discerning the intent of the Spirit. Peter went to Cornelius in response to the prompting of the Spirit ("the Spirit said to him" that there were three men that would take him to Cornelius in Acts 10:19), and it was when the leadership of the church in Antioch were in prayer and fasting that "the Holy Spirit said, 'Set apart for me Barnabas and Saul for the work to which I have called them'" (Acts 13:2), leading to their ministry in Asia Minor among Gentiles. The church was intentionally attentive to and responsive to the Spirit. What is noteworthy, of course, is that the Spirit called them to cross boundaries—cultural, ethnic, socioeconomic—that moved them beyond their immediate circle and propelled them to missional witness.

Finally, they received the Spirit, recognized the primacy of the Spirit, responded to the witness of the Spirit, and then, no surprise, they also *rejoiced* in the Spirit. The early church was a community of deep and palpable joy (Acts 2:46), and this joy is linked to the presence of the Spirit: "The disciples were filled with joy and with the Holy Spirit" (Acts 13:52). There is no avoiding the clear links that Luke makes between the presence of the Spirit and the resilient joy that marked the life of the church.

Thus we see that the Spirit who is clearly evident in the life and ministry of Jesus finds parallel expression in the life and ministry of the early church. The bridge between them is two defining events: the ascension of Christ Jesus and, ten days later, the outpouring of the Spirit on the day of Pentecost.

Let us consider, then, the dynamic between these two events and how to see them together so they can each inform the meaning of the other.

ASCENSION AND PENTECOST IN DYNAMIC COUNTERPOINT

The ascension represents the culmination of the earthly ministry of Jesus. In the moments before he ascends, he assures his disciples that he will return to his Father in triumphant expectation of the consummation of his kingdom. He blesses his disciples and calls them to the ministry of establishing the church and announcing the reign of God. The ascension confirms Christ Jesus as the benevolent Lord of the cosmos, the one in whom and through whom all things are reconciled to God. He has assumed flesh, encountered death, and triumphed over all that would destroy humanity and the created order. And now, in his full humanity, Jesus is at the right hand of the Father and is the Lord of all creation and the head of the church. The church lives and breathes as the people of God insofar as she is sustained in a dynamic and life-giving fellowship with her ascended Lord. Thus, in one respect, the ascension establishes the church, for she is the body of Christ, with Christ as her head (Ephesians 4:15-16).

But as Jesus anticipates his ascension, he urges his disciples to wait. They cannot do the ministry to which he calls them *except* in the grace and power of the Holy Spirit, the one for whom they are to wait. This means that Pentecost is an imperative. The purposes of God in Christ for the church and the world presume the outpouring of the gift of the Spirit at Pentecost. Pentecost is the essential consequence, one might say, of Christ's work—from incarnation to the cross to the resurrection and the ascension. It is not that these events are less significant. It is, rather, that without Pentecost the effect, the saving benefit, of these events is not fulfilled. Jesus therefore impresses on the disciples that they need to wait.

Pentecost, then, is not merely a bonus experience. It is not that with Pentecost we have something good but not essential. To the contrary, the ascension *must* be complemented by Pentecost. Christ Jesus only functions as Lord of the church, the cosmos, and the individual believer through the gift that is given on the day of Pentecost.

We are only able to enter into the salvation of God mediated to us in Christ through the grace of the Spirit. The objective work of God in Christ—incarnation, cross, resurrection, and ascension—is made present to us, and thus experienced in our lives and in our world, through the gift given on the day of Pentecost. Thus, to know Christ and be united with Christ—to, in the language of John 15:4, remain in him as he remains in us—happens through the grace of the Spirit. The apostle Paul puts this bluntly when he writes, "Anyone who does not have the Spirit of Christ does not belong to him" (Romans 8:9). This seems hard and uncompromising until we realize that it is in the very economy of God's salvation that the grace of God in Christ is known to us, in us, and in our world through the Spirit. Thus the risen Christ dwells in us, as Paul puts it, "through his Spirit that dwells in you" (Romans 8:11). Therefore, it is the Spirit that witnesses with our spirit that we are children of God (Romans 8:16). The apostle is simply affirming that Pentecost is essential, for only with Pentecost can we know the salvation of God.

This finds expression in our worship. Christian worship is christocentric in that the essential content of worship is the adoration of Christ Jesus as Savior and Lord. But it is also trinitarian in that we do this to the glory of God the Father (Philippians 2:11) in the grace and inspiration and empowerment of the Spirit. It is by the Spirit that we, as children of God, bring our unbounded praise and adoration to Christ.

It is by the Spirit that the church fulfills its identity and purpose—in worship, and also in Christian formation and in mission. For the church to be the church, Pentecost needed to happen. This is why Jesus urges his disciples to wait for the promised gift of God. His disciples will know what it means to receive the Spirit, recognize the work of the Spirit, respond to the Spirit, and rejoice in the Spirit so that they can truly be the people of God and the body of Christ in the world. And so they wait until the gift is given.

It is appropriate to ask, What does it mean that the Spirit was given? What are the implications? What difference did it make? Three things need to be affirmed. First, this gift was long foreseen—as Peter notes in his sermon on Pentecost—and is the culmination of God's redemptive work. This is the capstone of what God intended to do: God's very Spirit would animate the whole of creation with redemptive and healing grace. The Spirit of God would infuse the people of God and make them the tabernacle of God. Even more, God's Spirit would animate and transform each individual human person.

Second, this radical infusion could only happen when the alienation between God and the creation could be overcome— particularly the alienation between humanity and God. This was overcome with the incarnation, death, and resurrection-ascension of Christ.

But then, third, the full meaning of what happened at Pentecost will not be known until the ascended Christ is fully revealed. The Spirit was given as a promise of what is yet to come. The genius of our shared life now, our hope and the focus and discipline of our lives, is that we live now in light of Pentecost. This changes everything, even though the full implications will not be known until Christ is revealed. Those who are women and men of faith live under the benevolent authority of the ascended Lord Jesus Christ in the fullness of the Spirit with intentionality and purpose, knowing that there is more to come. But we must not overstate what has already happened with the gift of the Spirit. We continue to long for the coming of Christ and the full revelation of his grace and power. Confident of that day, we walk in and bear the fruit of the Spirit. Nothing quite states that we are a people confident in the purposes of God as that we live now in the Spirit that God has given us as promise, down payment, and gift.

And with Pentecost, we do not leave the ascension behind. We do not assume that we have come to a higher place or greater spiritual experience. Rather, the Spirit brings us into a fuller appreciation of the significance of the ascension: now we see clearly that Christ is risen, ascended, and the benevolent Lord of all. We see this in the experience of Stephen: in the power of the Spirit, at the very moment of his stoning, he sees the Son of Man at the right hand of God (Acts 7:55). That is, the Christ event is not behind us but ever *before* us. It is not that the Gospel of Luke was about Jesus and the book of Acts is about the Spirit. To the contrary, Acts is about the gift of the Spirit that equipped and empowered the church to preach Christ and worship Christ. Indeed, the apostle Paul insisted that his passion was none other than to "preach Christ and him crucified" (1 Corinthians 2:2). Thus it is fitting that the book of Acts ends with Paul in Rome, "proclaiming the kingdom of God and teaching about the Lord Jesus Christ" (Acts 28:31). That is the bottom line. It is done, of course, in the power of the Spirit, but that is precisely what the Spirit does: enable us to see Jesus, preach Jesus, and live lives of devotion and service to Jesus. Or, as Douglas Farrow puts it:

> His ascension is a vital part of his priestly work, and his priestly work leaves nothing untouched, because all that he commits to the Father is in turn handed over to the Spirit. . . . We must look . . . to the Spirit, whose task it is in the ascension to present Jesus to the Father as the beloved son and heir, and to present him to us also, in his heavenly session, as brother and Lord.[1]

---

[1]Douglas Farrow, *Ascension and Ecclesia: On the Significance of the Doctrine of the Ascension for Ecclesiology and Christian Cosmology* (Grand Rapids, MI: Eerdmans, 1999), 263-64, 266. Farrow establishes unequivocally the centrality of the ascension in our understanding of redemptive history and the meaning of the church, demonstrating on the one hand that we only understand Pentecost in light of the ascension and, in turn, that Pentecost is all about enabling us to enter into fellowship with the incarnate, crucified, ascended Lord.

By the grace of the Holy Spirit given at Pentecost, we are enabled to see, know, love, and live in fellowship with Christ Jesus. In other words, there is not a sequence from the Father to the Son to the Spirit. Rather, from the beginning all members of the Trinity were active in the redemptive purposes of God. This is evident, in part, in the obvious role of the Spirit in the coming of Christ. The Spirit superintended the events around the incarnation, then anointed and empowered Jesus throughout his ministry, all with the view that his disciples would follow him.

But we do not go beyond Jesus when we get to Pentecost; rather, the gift of the Spirit is the means for us to know the grace of God in Christ. Our faith remains radically christocentric. Our vision is Christ ascended; that vision now becomes an existential reality in our lives through the gift of Pentecost. The church now lives in dynamic communion, in real time, with her ascended Lord.

Jesus Christians and Spirit Christians?

Thus, ascension and Pentecost are necessarily twinned. They are distinct events in redemptive history, but each is only known and only makes sense in the light of the other.

But all too frequently, Christians focus on one at the expense of the other. Some Christians never seem to get to Pentecost. The Holy Spirit is, at best, a secondary figure; Pentecost is an event of the distant past that has no influence in their lives and in the life of the church. Not only is Pentecost Sunday not observed, the Spirit is hardly mentioned either in public worship or in their personal lives and conversations. They are *Jesus* Christians: they affirm and worship Christ risen and ascended; they live intentionally as followers of Jesus. They might even be a bit suspicious of any "Spirit-talk" by those who have a sense of the *immediacy* of the Spirit in their lives, work, and ministry. They downplay references to the Spirit so much that the Spirit is at best incidental in worship, prayer, and witness. In principle, they are trinitarian; they affirm the three persons in perfect unity, and they recognize that the Spirit was sent by God and brings about the purposes of God in the church and the world. But the Spirit is not an *immediate* presence or power. The Spirit's work is always mediated—through either Scripture (for Protestant Christians) or through the church hierarchy (for Catholic Christians). For many evangelical Protestant Christians, the Spirit was active in the inspiration and writing of Scripture but now, with the Bible in hand, there is no need for an immediacy of the Spirit. Some Christians, it seems, never truly get to Pentecost.

Others, though, definitely get to Pentecost, but the ascension is left in the rearview mirror. They are what we might call "Spirit" Christians. It is evident in their worship, their language—the way that they speak about their spiritual experience—and in their approach to life, work, and ministry. It is all about the Spirit. For them, the high point in the church calendar is Pentecost Sunday. Jesus came, of course, but to the end that God's people would be baptized with the Holy Spirit and fire! (Matthew 3:11). For all practical purposes, Jesus has become the distant figure—happy with developments, but not immediately present to the church and almost a secondary figure. Their worship and experience has become Spirit-centered.

Neither of these groups is truly trinitarian. They may well speak the language of the Trinity and affirm that Father, Son, and Holy Spirit are three persons, one God, for all of eternity. Yet the first are more "binitarian" than trinitarian, in that the Spirit is hardly a significant factor in their lives and worship. And for the second, the Son—and the Father as well—are secondary figures, at best. These are people for whom "God" is synonymous with "the Holy Spirit."

The witness of the New Testament and the history of the church suggests that our faith is only truly Christian if we are indeed trinitarian, affirming the full deity of the Father, Son, and Spirit, and that our visceral orientation is toward Christ—that is, that our faith is trinitarian and christocentric. We are only truly "in Christ" when we live as the church and as Christians fully "in the Spirit." When we do not get to Pentecost, the experience of Jesus in Luke and of the church in the book of Acts are somewhat foreign to us, and the full benefits of the ascension are not known in our lives, bodies, relationships, and work. If we are focused on Christ but have no immediate sense of the Spirit through Pentecost:

- We are biblicists who see Scripture as an end in itself rather than a revelation of the risen and ascended Christ.

- We typically are overdependent on human strategies for personal and church development rather than responsive to the immediacy of the Spirit's guidance.

- We are overly dependent on structures of authority, which, while important and essential, are often a means of control that is inattentive to how the Spirit is speaking through those at the margins of the community.

- We as often as not lack an appreciation of the emotional character of "life in the Spirit"—and thus are inattentive to the vital place of joy and consolation in Christian experience and worship.

On the other hand, something else goes terribly askew when we become "spirit-Christians" and lose the anchor and vision of the ascended Christ. As often as not, those of us who are "pneumo-centered" rather than Christ-centered and Spirit empowered are marked by another set of characteristics[2]:

- We do not take seriously the careful exposition of Scripture along with the vital place of baptism and the Lord's Supper in the life of the church.

- We typically equate the presence of the Spirit with positive and happy feelings rather than appreciating how the Spirit is present to the church in both blessing and suffering, in both joy and lament.

- The focus is often on the person of charismatic figures rather than on the presence and glory of Christ.[3]

- There is sometimes an undue fascination with the demonic such that all manner of simple human predicaments and challenges are attributed to demonic activity.

But the good news is that we do not need to choose. The answer to a truncated pneumatology is not a pneumo-centric worship or experience. We do not correct an imbalance with another imbalance. Our faith is radically Christ-centered; Christ is the focus, vision, orientation, and commitment of the church. Yet we can only truly be Christ-centered if we cultivate a full and indeed radical openness to the Spirit. We can set our eyes on Jesus, the

---

[2] I published a full essay considering this contrast: "Christ Centred or Spirit Centred?: Why the Question Matters; Why the Answer Makes all the Difference," *CRUX* (Fall 2019): 19-28.

[3] Christian leaders of this orientation tend to legitimize themselves with their followers by noting how many miracles or demonstrations of unusual grace and power are associated with their ministry or their congregation, but this is very much not what the apostle Paul did. Instead, what marked his ministry and gave it legitimacy was his radical identification with the cross of Christ. See especially his autobiographical reflections in 2 Corinthians where he observes, "We have this treasure in clay jars. . . . We are afflicted in every way . . . always carrying in the body the death of Jesus, so that the life of Jesus may also be visible in our bodies. . . . So death is at work in us, but life in you" (2 Corinthians 4:7-12).

author and finisher of our faith (Hebrews 12:2), and do so with deep and intentional attentiveness to the Spirit, a thorough dependency on the Spirit, and the humility of knowing the inner witness of the Spirit that witnesses with our spirit that we are children of God (Romans 8:16).

Can we cultivate an understanding of the Spirit that is truly trinitarian and that, in turn, leads us to a dynamic awareness of the presence of the Spirit in worship, witness, joy, and sorrow, in seasons of blessing and times of difficulty and suffering? Can we at least approximate something of what we see in the life of Jesus in the Gospel of Luke and in the experience of the early church in Acts? This is the goal of what follows: to call for a greater attentiveness to the Spirit, not as something that would replace Christ as the focus but as that which brings us into the presence of the living and ascended Christ Jesus. It is to this end that we pray, "Welcome, Holy Spirit."

CHAPTER TWO

THE SPIRIT IN THE
GOSPEL OF JOHN

One with the Father and with the Son

M Y BASIC ASSUMPTION is that our theology and experience of the Holy Spirit need to be thoroughly trinitarian. A clear and proper understanding of the Trinity is the essential reference for anything we say about the Holy Spirit. Indeed, seeing and appreciating the Trinity opens our eyes to understanding and embracing the role of the Spirit in the church, in the redemption of the world, and in our own personal lives. With this in mind, let us consider the witness to the Spirit in the Gospel of John, another foundational text for our understanding of the Holy Spirit.

The Holy Spirit is prominent in this Gospel. The opening chapter includes the promise that, just as the Spirit descended like a dove on Jesus, even so he would baptize his disciples with the Holy Spirit (John 1:32-33). The image of the dove is complemented by the metaphor of wind in John 3, where we have the affirmation from Jesus that those who come to him are reborn from above, born of water and Spirit, and blow where the Spirit, or the wind, blows. This metaphor emerges again at the conclusion of the book, where Jesus blows on his disciples and calls on them to receive the gift of the Spirit (John 20:21-22). His commission to them—"as the

Father has sent me, so I send you"—is fulfilled in the grace and power of the Spirit.

Another metaphor for the Spirit arises in John 4 and 7, where Jesus speaks of living water—not the water of the well, which occasions his conversation with the Samaritan woman, but the water that satisfies the deepest yearning of the human soul (John 4:14). Later, in John 7, we see confirmed that this reference to living or running water is an allusion to the Spirit.

But most crucial for our understanding of the Spirit is that in reading the Gospel of John we are drawn into the wonder of what it means to call God *triune*. The only Spirit we know and experience is the Spirit who is one with the Father and the Son. Here is where the aptly called "upper room discourse" of John 14–16 plays such a pivotal place in our understanding.

Jesus opens by speaking to his disciples about his upcoming departure—bringing them into the wonder of redemptive history that includes the culmination of his earthly ministry. He will be moving from this discourse to the cross; he assures them of his resurrection and advises them that he will be returning to the Father, from whom he has come. Jesus then reminds them that he is the vine and that they are the branches (John 15:5). Their life is bound up in his life; they abide in him and he abides in them (John 15:4). Jesus no doubt says this in anticipation of the ascension; it is even with, if not actually *because* of, the ascension that they can live in union with him.

This union with Christ is only possible through the work of the Spirit, but we still must begin with the ascension and the call to union with Christ. This is our baseline for any consideration of the work and ministry of the Spirit. It is our guide through the challenging issues and complexities of a theology of the Holy

Spirit. And we must recognize that this perspective is not unique to John. All that is witnessed to in John about the character of the Christian life is echoed in Paul's epistles and in the book of Hebrews. Thus, in John we have the call to "abide in me as I abide in you"—a theme in John (see John 6, for example). And Paul can speak of "Christ in you, the hope of glory" (Colossians 1:27) and how, therefore, the goal of his ministry is to present each one mature in Christ (Colossians 1:28-29). The epistle to the Ephesians opens with a paean that celebrates the wonder that "in Christ" all things are created, all things are redeemed, and all things find their goal and meaning, including the life of the individual Christian. Later in Ephesians, he writes that we—as the church—grow and mature as we grow up into him who is the head of the church, Christ Jesus.

To be a Christian is to be found *in Christ*; there is no graduating beyond Jesus and no experience in the Christian life that surpasses this. Notice, for example, the poignancy of the apostle's words in the book of Philippians when he speaks of the deep yearning of his own heart: to know Christ and the power of his resurrection, even if he shares in the sufferings of Christ (Philippians 3:10-11). There is no experience of God beyond that found in Christ Jesus. This simply cannot be overstated. The central and defining figure of the Gospel of John, from beginning to end, is Jesus. He is the eternal Logos through whom all things are created (John 1:1), and at the culmination of the Gospel of John it is Christ engaging his disciples—as their Lord, Master, Healer, and Friend— that captures the imagination. Our deepest yearning is to encounter Christ; our hope and our healing is found in meeting Christ—to know him, love him, serve him, and to be found in him. Saying all of this does not for a moment diminish the significance of the Spirit in our lives, in the church, and in the world. Rather, it is a reminder that we *locate* the Spirit's ministry within a christocentric faith.

THE HOLY SPIRIT AND THE TRIUNITY OF GOD

With this vision clearly before us, we can consider what is surely the great chapter on the Trinity in Scripture: John 14. All of Scripture is holy ground, but one almost has the sense that this is the holy of holies. Here, in this breathtaking vision of the God who is three and the three who are one, we enter into the heart of the universe.

The Trinity is not revealed here through philosophical argument and an exercise of logic, though this is certainly presumed. Rather, we have described for us a dynamic movement of going and coming, of one going and other coming as the other is sent. The Trinity is not revealed as a complicated mathematical formula—three and one and one and three. Rather, we see a dynamic movement of Father, Son, and Spirit in perfect harmony. What is assumed throughout, of course, is the profound unity of God; monotheism anchors our vision of life and work and ministry, our knowledge of the salvation of God, and the mission of God in the world. There is only one God. And yet, this one God is revealed as three persons—first Jesus speaks of his relationship with the Father, and, second, he announces that the Spirit will be sent.

Jesus and the Father. John 14 opens with Jesus speaking about his mission and his relationship with the Father. He tells the disciples that he will be returning to the Father. Philip is perplexed, but makes the obvious request: "Show us the Father" (John 14:8). Then Jesus stresses as powerfully and poignantly as anywhere in

Scripture that he is the revelation of the Father—if you believe in God, believe in him. Jesus and the Father are one. They are distinct, and yet to know one is to know the other. Jesus is going into the presence of the Father, and in speaking of this movement—the ascension—Jesus shows his disciples that he and the Father are in perfect fellowship.

This dynamic between the Father and the Son is the true home of the disciples. Jesus promises them that where he will be they will be—in the generative and life-giving space where the Father and the Son abide in perfect unity. We are drawn into the wonder that the Father and the Son are distinct but inseparable: "Jesus said to [Thomas], 'I am the way, and the truth, and the life. No one comes to the Father except through me. If you know me, you will know my Father also. From now on you do know him and have seen him. . . . Believe me that I am in the Father and the Father is in me'" (John 14:6-7, 11a).

Then we learn that the relationship between Jesus and the Father is marked by love and obedience: Jesus loves and is loved by the Father; he does the will of the Father, deferring to the will of the one who sent him (John 14:31). But further, Jesus speaks of his work, and we see that his mission is quite simply to make the Father known. In other words, John's Gospel affirms the completeness and comprehensiveness of God's self-revelation in Jesus Christ.

Jesus and the Spirit. Then we come to the focus for our reflections here—the vision of the third person of the Trinity. Until about halfway through John 14, I can see the disciples thinking and discussing among themselves, "Oh, so there are two of them!"—Father and Son, both fully and equally God. Their faith, at this point, is binitarian. But just as they come to appreciate this,

Jesus now speaks of another, the "Paraclete," whom the Father will send in Jesus' name. It begins to dawn on the disciples that there are not two but three! There is *another* who is very God of very God.

Now Jesus speaks of the Spirit as the third person who will be sent even as Jesus was sent. The Spirit is an Advocate, but not an advocate in the same way as Jesus. The Spirit is not a one-to-one replacement for Jesus; the Spirit is the essential *complement* and *counterpart* to Jesus. Thus, in the same way that we speak of the Father and the Son as distinct but inseparable, the Son and the Spirit are distinct yet you cannot separate either from the other. To know the Spirit is to know the Son whom the Spirit points to and glorifies. The Spirit becomes the *essential* means by which all that Jesus has accomplished in the incarnation, cross, and ascension is revealed in the world and fulfilled in the world. Union with Christ and fellowship with the Trinity is only possible through the Holy Spirit.

John Calvin articulates this beautifully. On the one hand, he stresses that union with Christ is the only means by which we know the benefits that would come to us through Christ and through his suffering. "He had to become ours and to dwell within us;" we had to be "'engrafted into him" [Rom. 11:17], and to 'put on Christ' [Gal. 3:27]."[1] Faith is the means by which we enter into this grace—no surprise from Calvin—but then we must not miss Calvin's insistence on "the Holy Spirit as the bond that unites us to Christ."[2] The giving of the Spirit at Pentecost is essential to the capacity of the church to know the salvation of

---

[1] John Calvin, *Institutes of the Christian Religion*, ed. John T. McNeill, trans. Ford Lewis Battles (Louisville, KY: Westminster John Knox Press, 2011), 3.1.1 (537).
[2] Calvin, *Institutes*, 3.1.1 (537).

God and to live in fellowship with God the Father, God the Son, and God the Holy Spirit.

The Spirit is an advocate who comes alongside, but John also speaks of the Spirit as one who lives in us, abiding in us (John 14:17b). This suggests, of course, that if the vision of John 15:4 is to be made complete—abiding in Christ as Christ abides in us—it will be as we respond to the ministry of the Holy Spirit. And then, also, Jesus makes two statements that surely are parallel affirmations. He declares, "My peace I give to you" (John 14:27), and in the same moment and in conjunction with this peace, he speaks of "the Advocate, the Holy Spirit, whom the Father will send in my name." To know the peace of God, we welcome the Spirit into our lives as advocate and indweller.

Here I might mention the "filioque" controversy. In the ancient church, Greek or Eastern theologians insisted that the Spirit proceeds from the Father directly. For the Latin and Western theologians, the Spirit comes from the Father *and* the Son (thus the Latin for the reference to the son—the *filio*) with a clear sense that the procession of the Spirit is a christological event. The resolution, as many observe, is to use the language of "through" as a way to affirm that there is indeed a single source or origin (the Father) and that the gift of the Spirit is mediated to us through the person and work of the Son.

However, it was one thing for this to be understood. It was another when French monks in Jerusalem actually inserted "and the Son" into the Nicene Creed, which had originated from the Council of Nicaea in the early fourth century. This became a common addition for the church in the West. Things came to a head when in 1014 Pope Benedict VIII formalized its use as part of the creed in the Western church. This addition was deeply offensive to the Eastern church and, in 1054, after many back-and-forths, the Western and Eastern patriarchs excommunicated one another.

At the heart of this debate is the specifics of how the Spirit draws us into and is present to us as an active participant in the Trinity. The Western church has sought to maintain that the work of the Spirit is mediated to us through Christ. As noted in the introduction, I have chosen to use the original text of the Nicene Creed, without the *filioque* clause. However, we can lean into the language of John 14 where the source of all things, the Father, is the one who sends the Spirit. But we can qualify this, as the text does, with the affirmation that the Spirit is given in the light of and through the one who is the Son and by virtue of the work and ministry of the Son.

The Wisdom of Ambrose of Milan and the Early Church

How then do we speak of the Spirit? How can we have an understanding of the Spirit as one who is the third member of the Trinity? What does it mean for us to affirm that the Spirit who is sent by the Father, through the Son, is one with the Father and the Son?

One of the most helpful ways to read John 14 and respond to this question is by drawing on the wisdom of early church voices. Doing so helps us appreciate how foundational this great trinitarian chapter is to our understanding and experience of the Spirit. This means that we read John 14 in light of the ancient creeds, most notably the Nicene Creed. This was the foundational benchmark in trinitarian theology, witness, and worship, the product of theologians and writers from East and West wrestling with the full significance of what it meant to call God triune and thereby worship God in truth—what it is, precisely, that John 14 is revealing to us.

We could turn to any number of voices, but I am choosing here to appeal to fourth-century bishop and theologian Ambrose of Milan. I do so largely because he comes to the great trinitarian questions through a consideration of what it means to speak of the Holy Spirit as one with the Father and the Son. As with all his peers, the creed established the point of departure for understanding God and the purposes of God in Christ and the Spirit. Ambrose leveraged the affirmation of the creed, and in his "On the Holy Spirit" probed the relationship between Christ and the Spirit, but particularly focused on how the Spirit is God *with* the Father and the Son.

Ambrose first affirms that the Holy Spirit is very God of very God.[3] He mentions, for example, that the Spirit has the power and capacity to forgive sin.[4] And, as with the Father and the Son, the Spirit is Light.[5] Then he stresses that we cannot separate the Father, the Son, and the Spirit. To have one is to have all three. They function and minister with perfect unity and harmony. But while they are one, they are also distinct; they are not commingled.[6] He observes, for example, that their roles are different; he notes in particular that the Spirit is the one who anoints, and even Christ was anointed by the Spirit.[7] But though they have different roles,

---

[3]Ambrose of Milan, "Three Books of St. Ambrose on the Holy Spirit," in *St. Ambrose: Select Works and Letters*, ed. Philip Schaff and Henry Wace, A Select Library of the Nicene and Post-Nicene Fathers of the Christian Church, Second Series, vol. 10 (New York: Christian Literature Company, 1896), 1.7.81; 1.14.168.
[4]Ambrose, "On the Holy Spirit," 1.10.112.
[5]Ambrose, "On the Holy Spirit," 1.14.164.
[6]Ambrose, "On the Holy Spirit," 1.9.106.
[7]Ambrose, "On the Holy Spirit," 1.9.

the Holy Spirit is God with the Father and the Son—indeed, there is no division in the Godhead but rather a fundamental unity: "the unity remains undivided, since neither can Christ be without the Spirit, nor the Spirit without Christ, for the unity of the divine nature cannot be divided."[8] Thus, for Ambrose: "Equality excludes confusion; unity excludes separation."[9]

Then, having affirmed the equality and unity of the three persons, Ambrose speaks to the distinctive identity and role of the Spirit. In their relationship with each other within the Trinity, the Spirit is the *fount* of the Father and the Son.[10] The Father is the fount of life: the Father gave, as Ambrose puts it, "the very prerogative of the Divine Nature."[11] The Son is the fount with the Father; he receives all things from the Father, and what the Spirit communicates is from the Son.[12] All the while, Ambrose insists that "the Father is in the Son, and the Son in the Father, so the Spirit of God and the Spirit of Christ are both in the Father and in the Son."[13] But then, while the Father and the Son sent the Spirit, Ambrose notes that the Father and the Spirit sent the Son! Thus he concludes: "If, then, the Son and the Spirit send each other, as the Father sends, there is no inferiority of subjection, but a community of power."[14]

Fundamentally, echoing the language of John 14, the work of the Spirit is to glorify the Son: "The Spirit is said to hear from the Father, and to glorify the Son . . . who is the image of the invisible God and the brightness of God's glory."[15] Further, Ambrose

---

[8]Ambrose, "On the Holy Spirit," 3.7.44.
[9]Ambrose, "On the Holy Spirit," 3.16.116.
[10]Ambrose, "On the Holy Spirit," 1.15.172.
[11]Ambrose, "On the Holy Spirit," 3.16.116.
[12]Ambrose, "On the Holy Spirit," 2.12.134.
[13]Ambrose, "On the Holy Spirit," 3.1.6.
[14]Ambrose, "On the Holy Spirit," 3.1.8.
[15]Ambrose, "On the Holy Spirit," 2.12.138.

stresses that the work of the Spirit is linked to but not limited to the Word; the power of God comes in the interplay of Word and Spirit. "Since then," he writes, "the Sword of the Word is the Holy Spirit, and the Sword of the Holy Spirit is the Word of God, there is certainly in Them oneness of power."[16]

THE ANCIENT HERESIES

Why does all of this matter? Why do we need to listen to Ambrose as a representative of those who would help our generation make sense of the creedal affirmation of the Spirit as one with the Father and the Son? It is because only with clarity about the unity, equality, and distinct roles of the three persons of the Trinity do we have the foundation to respond to perspectives on the Spirit that are not consistent with what we mean when we declare that we believe in one God as Father, Son, and Holy Spirit.

Ambrose—almost pedantically, one might say—goes on and on about the Trinity because he has a particular challenge. He is taking on two heresies at the same time. First, he is challenging the Arians, who in the Milan of his day had control of more than one major church. The Arians are best known for their denial of the full divinity of Christ. For them, there is only one who could properly be spoken of as "God"—the one we know to be the Father. The Son was a lower being. And since it is typically the case that the conviction of the deity of the Spirit flows from our understanding of the deity of the Son, it is no surprise that for the Arians the Spirit is not a person and definitely not God in the same sense as the Father. The Eunomians were what some think of as extreme Arians. They not only saw Christ as not divine, but also saw the

---

[16]Ambrose, "On the Holy Spirit," 3.7.47.

Spirit as in a sense the "glory" of Christ—not a distinct person and definitely not very God of very God.

So the Arian vision of God is what we might speak of as a *descending* staircase: the Father is very God of very God. The Son is a created being—a tremendously important being, yet still not very God of very God. The Spirit is merely a force or "presence," but, again, definitely not God and at best only derivative of the Son.

Second, Ambrose took on the Sabellians, who were modalist in their approach to the Trinity. That is, they did not believe in a Holy Trinity of three persons but rather that there is only one who is God, and that God is revealed in different modes: first as Father, then as Son, and then, as the ultimate and culminating revelation, as Spirit. Each is an improvement on the other, so that the Spirit then becomes the ultimate expression of God in the world. Jesus, as a human figure, is in the past, and now the church and the Christian live in the fullness of the Spirit. The Sabellian vision of God is an *ascending* staircase. We begin with the Father, and the Son is a step up, a fuller revelation of God—but the Spirit is the ultimate and longed-for revelation of God in the world and thus in the church.

To summarize, for the Arians and their cousins the Eunomians, only God (that is, the Father) is very God of very God. The Son, while special, is not God in the same sense, and the Spirit is not a person, not God. For the Sabellians, it was the reverse: the Spirit is the ultimate expression of God, the culmination of the revelation of God as God.

For Ambrose, both are wrong; neither is truly trinitarian. The genius of Ambrose and of other voices from both the Western and Eastern churches—Gregory of Nyssa, for example—was to insist on the trinitarian vision of God and of the redemptive purposes of God. They insisted on the *triunity* of God as a constant referent in Christian worship and witness, so that when we think and pray and respond to the Holy Spirit, the only Spirit we know is the Spirit who is one with the Father and the Son. Thus they would defend the church from both the Arians and the Sabellians at the same time.

THE CONTEMPORARY CHALLENGE

Both of these heresies—the Arians-Eunomians and the Sabellians—have their counterparts in the church today. We might not want to use an inflammatory word such as "heresy" to describe them, but the study of the ancient heresies helps us be attentive, keep our bearings, and stay the course. The genius of Ambrose was that he did not try to correct a heresy with a heresy. He did not correct the Sabellians by standing with the Arians; rather, he insisted that neither was truly trinitarian. It is not uncommon for us to try to correct an imbalance by overemphasizing the other end of the spectrum. But when we overreact or overcompensate, we never get it right. An example of this is Protestants who have rejected the sacramentalism of the Catholic church and become *anti-sacramental.* This is no solution when the New Testament so clearly calls the church to a sacramental faith. In our current climate, there is a legitimate concern about church communities that have not developed a full-orbed theology of the Spirit that informs worship, formation, and mission. They have, one might say, a truncated pneumatology. And some then suggest that we need to press the other way and *overemphasize* the Spirit. But an overcorrection is not a correction.

Or consider the example of the Reformers, notably Luther and Calvin. They were rightly dismayed with the so-called enthusiasts of their day, who neglected the Scriptures and lived by immediate impressions that they attributed to the voice and witness of the Spirit. The Reformers, understandably but unfortunately, ended up denying any sense of the immediate presence of the Spirit in the life of the church. The solution, of course, with Ambrose of Milan and the early church, is to ground our faith and experience in the triune character of the Living God, Father, Son, and Spirit. This is our baseline. We affirm the Trinity as a communion of persons, a fellowship sustained by love. Theologians commonly speak of the *social* Trinity to describe the deep mutuality within the Father, the Son, and the Spirit: the mutuality, the interpenetration and intercommunion, the sharing of life between the three members of the Trinity.

This needs to be complemented by an appreciation of what is typically spoken of as the *economic* Trinity, which considers how the Trinity works, both in creation and in redemption: that all things originate in the Father, all things are mediated through the Son, and all things are effective in the world by the Spirit. The Father is the source of life—whether in creation or in redemption. The Son is the *mediator* through whom all things have been created and through whom all things are made new. The Spirit is the *executor*—the one by whom the creation comes into being and by whom we know God's salvation. All the work of the triune God begins with the Father, is mediated through the Son, and is effected in the world by the Spirit. We know God as one who has self-revealed in in creation and redemption. We see the ways in which the Spirit glorifies the Son who, in turn, glorifies the Father. Further, we must speak of this trinitarian perspective when we consider creation, not just salvation. The Bible affirms that the Son, the second person of the Trinity, was the one *through* whom all things were created. We cannot speak of the Father as Creator and the Son as Redeemer. That would be a false distinction. Both were involved in creation; both are involved in salvation. And, of course, the same principle would apply to the work of the Holy Spirit. Any other perspective would be a subtle, if not explicit, tritheism (a belief in three gods). The affirmation of the Scriptures and the ancient creeds is that there is one God who exists eternally in three persons. Consequently, no member of the Trinity can act independently. God is one. Every act of God is of necessity the act of all three.

Who, then, saves? All three, of course. Salvation is the work of the whole Trinity functioning in perfect harmony. Salvation finds its origin with the Father. We are saved through the mediatorial work of the Son who continues to exercise the authority of the Father and continues to intercede for us. And the Spirit grants us new birth and transforms us into the image of Christ.

Therefore, the Father is known through Jesus Christ. There is only one God and Father of humanity—the God revealed through Jesus. Similarly, there is only one Christ—the Christ who is known through the illuminating work of the Spirit. Apart from the Spirit, we cannot know Christ. Christ saves and redeems *through* the Spirit. It is by the Spirit that we are born again to new life. It is by the Spirit that we are transformed and made new, and by the Spirit we mature in our faith. It is by the Spirit that the Christian community, the church, is built up and established in Christ. Consequently, any theology that separates Christ and the Spirit violates something that is fundamental to the character and work of the triune God. Though triune, God cannot be separated; and though triune, God works as Father, Son, and Spirit in perfect harmony. The genius of a dynamic theology of the Trinity is holding both in tension—both the social Trinity (the communion and harmony of three persons) and the economic Trinity (the dynamic of all things coming from the Father through the Son and known in the world through the grace of the Spirit).

Ambrose concludes that our faith requires an appreciation of the Trinity, and that "the coherence of your soul is lessened if you do not believe in the unity of the Godhead in the Trinity."[17] He insists that we need to be intentional in this regard—not merely in our doctrinal affirmations, but in our liturgy and worship. If everything rests on embracing a trinitarian faith, then we need to affirm this again and again in our prayers and in our common worship.

This is why Ambrose's preaching and hymns were so intentional in affirming the unity of the Spirit and the holiness of the Spirit *with* the Father and the Son. As Ambrose puts it, the seraphim of Isaiah 6 say "Holy, Holy, Holy" not once or twice but three times, for "even in a hymn you may understand the distinction of Persons in the Trinity, and the oneness of the Godhead, and while they say this they proclaim God."[18]

Some may ask if it is appropriate to pray directly to the Spirit, or if our prayers should always be addressed to the Father through the Son and by the Spirit. Our default prayer is no doubt to the Father, through the Son, in the Spirit. And yet, within faith and worship that is intentionally trinitarian, it is appropriate to directly invoke the Spirit as a way to affirm the place of the Spirit in the Trinity and give the Spirit proper place in the church. The Spirit, with the Father and the Son, is also an object of worship and prayer. Indeed, our only hope is if the Spirit would hear our

---

[17]Ambrose, "On the Holy Spirit," 3.3.14.
[18]Ambrose, "On the Holy Spirit," 3.16.110.

prayer and be present to us. But any prayer to the Spirit, such as "Come, Holy Spirit, come," must be against this backdrop of the triune character of God.

THE HOLY SPIRIT AS PERSON

Finally, the Holy Spirit is not only fully God with the Father and the Son, the Spirit is a person with the Father and the Son—not a mere force or power, but a person. The Spirit is more than merely the presence of God. The Spirit is very God of very God—a person distinct from the Father and the Son, though united with the Father and the Son. Maintaining this conviction keeps us from much that muddies the waters of our under-standing and experience.

Because of the language of wind so often associated with the Spirit, it is perhaps understandable that there is an inclination to depersonalize the Spirit. But we need to be alert to language or hymnody that suggests that the Spirit is some vague force, even if "it" seems to be a redemptive or healing force. All too easily, this "power" can be spoken of as a kind of end in itself—something perhaps to own in its own right, rather than the presence and person of God. This is a subtle way of speaking of the Spirit as an impersonal force or presence rather than as a person.

We do not want power or presence or even, as it is often put, "manifest presence," in themselves. We want the person of the Holy Spirit, who brings us into fellowship with Christ. Yes, we long for the grace and empowerment of God, but we pray "Come, Holy Spirit, come" not that we might know power per se, or manifest presence, or that we would have some kind of dramatic experience or energy that alters the mood in the room. We pray so that we would know Christ and have more of Christ.

It is also not uncommon for some, following Augustine, to speak of the Spirit as the love between the Father and the Son.[19] There is much that commends this emphasis. However, Clark Pinnock rightly insists that the Spirit is more than this. We can appreciate that the Spirit plays a distinctive role within the Trinity, and that this might be spoken of as love. But when we speak of the Spirit as the "bond of love," we might inadvertently minimize the distinctive and personal identity of the Spirit. In other words, the Spirit is not merely "added" to the central dynamic of the Trinity—the counterpoint between the Father and the Son. Rather, the Spirit is a distinct person from Father and Son, no less part of the essence of the triunity of God with the Father and the Son.[20]

This is a further reminder that it is important to be attentive to pronouns. In the New Testament, *pneuma* ("spirit") is gender neutral. Yet John 16:13-14 uses a masculine pronoun where a neuter pronoun would normally appear—and one might wonder if this is a way by which Jesus through John intentionally highlights the personality of the Spirit. In the history of the church, many have chosen to portray the Spirit through female or feminine imagery—building perhaps on the language of Jesus himself where he compares the Spirit to a mother who brings about new life and new birth (John 3:5-6). In both cases, the main point is that the Spirit is another who, while not the same as Jesus, is of a similar kind: a person within the Holy Trinity. The Spirit relates to the Christian and to the church in a profoundly *personal*

---

[19]Augustine puts it this way: "According to the holy scriptures this Holy Spirit is not just the Father's alone nor the Son's alone, but the Spirit of them both, and thus he suggests to us the common charity by which the Father and the Son love each other." Saint Augustine, *The Trinity*, trans. Edmund Hill, ed. John E. Rotelle (New York: New City Press 1991), 421.
[20]Clark H. Pinnock, *Flame of Love: A Theology of the Holy Spirit* (Downers Grove, IL: Inter-Varsity Press, 1996), 38-39.

way—not as a vague force or presence, but a person who convicts of sin, leads into truth, teaches, comforts, calls, and anoints. This affirmation is foundational to Christian spirituality. When we refer to the Spirit as "presence," we easily lose a true sense of what it means to engage the Spirit as person.

We also need to resist conflating the human spirit with the divine spirit, speaking as though they are virtually or experientially one and the same. We must keep them distinct so we can appreciate that, in the language of the apostle Paul, "that very Spirit bear[s] witness with our spirit" (Romans 8:16). There is a deep synergy between the Spirit and our inner selves, but our only hope for union with Christ is that the Spirit of Christ would engage our sin-sick souls and draw us to Christ. Thus we must insist that the Spirit of Christ is other— an exterior and divine Spirit that engages our spirits as one who is God and comes from God, who witnesses to the Father and the Son and comes from the Father and the Son.

And to this person who is other, who is very God of very God, this Advocate and Comforter, we pray and ask for grace in our time of need. In our worship and witness, with our vision formed and informed by the triunity of God, who in Christ has acted and is acting in our world, we can pray: "Come, Holy Spirit, come." When we pray this prayer, we call to the one who is one with the Father and the Son and who draws us into fellowship with Christ. We can have a full knowledge and experience of the Spirit, not as a lesser being or as the ultimate expression of divine life, but as one—as the Gospel of John highlights and to whom Ambrose of Milan testifies—who with the Father and the Son is glorified and active in creation and redemption.

CHAPTER THREE

THE SPIRIT AND CREATION

*T*HERE IS AN INTRIGUING REFERENCE in Psalm 104 that might almost be seen as a passing reference but, on further reflection, must be not only noted but appreciated as significant. The psalmist is celebrating the glory and beauty of creation in exquisite detail, and then adds:

> When you send forth your spirit, they are created;
> and you renew the face of the ground. (Ps 104:30)

As has been made clear in previous chapters, our theology of the Spirit must be clear on the relationship of Pentecost to the ascension as well as the relationship of the Spirit within the Trinity to the Father and the Son. Later, we will consider personal experience—what it means for the Christian to know the gift of the Spirit and walk in the Spirit. And I will later speak to what it means to be the church that knows the grace of the immediacy of the Spirit in worship, governance, and mission.

But we must not miss the relationship of the Spirit to creation. The Spirit that empowers the church is the same Spirit who animates all living things and who, in turn, is revealed to us through the beauty of the creation. Yet all too frequently this dimension of pneumatology is overlooked or not given adequate attention. We have often failed to appreciate that a full appreciation of the work of the Spirit in redemption requires the foundational perspective of seeing and appreciating the Spirit as the *Spiritus Creator*. Clark Pinnock states this well:

> There has been neglect of the cosmic dimension of the Spirit's operations. . . . So much more attention has been given to the Spirit's work in redemption than the Spirit's work in creation. . . . We have read the Bible for its spiritual truth and neglected the material dimensions of its message. We have not emphasized that the Spirit who gives us life in Christ Jesus first gave life to our mortal bodies. Neglect of the cosmic dimension does harm. It minimizes the divine indwelling of the whole world, it reduces salvation to half size by attending to disembodied souls, it fosters forgetfulness about God's concern for ecology, etc. Neglect of the cosmic functions of the Spirit has consequences.[1]

Taking Pinnock's exhortation to heart, we can affirm that all considerations of the ministry of the Spirit assume and build on the witness of the Scriptures to the presence and power of the Spirit in creation. Indeed, we will not have a truly biblical understanding of the Spirit unless we have clarity in our appreciation of the Spirit as, specifically, the creator Spirit. The ministry of the Holy Spirit in the Christian and in the church needs to be seen against the backdrop of the cosmic work of God and its deep materiality. Only when we see the presence and power of the Spirit in the stuff of creation can we properly appreciate the ways in which the church and the Christian are truly "in the Spirit."

SPIRITUS CREATOR

When we ask what on earth the Spirit is doing, we begin by observing that the Spirit was an active player at the dawn of creation.

---

[1] Clark Pinnock, "The Role of the Spirit in Creation," *Asbury Theological Journal* 52, no. 1 (Spring 1997), 49.

Genesis 1 opens with the declaration: "In the beginning when God created the heavens and the earth, the earth was a formless void and darkness covered the face of the deep, while a wind from God swept over the face of the waters" (Genesis 1:1-2).

The Spirit did not suddenly arrive on the scene at Pentecost. As noted already, the Spirit was active in the birth, life, and ministry of Jesus. But we need to go back even further to be drawn into an appreciation of the cosmic purposes of God at creation itself and then, as we saw earlier in Psalm 104:30, in the ongoing renewal and restoration of the creation. We come to see that Pentecost is not merely about saving individuals or forming a church community. Ultimately, it is about the renewal and restoration of all things. The same Spirit who hovered over the waters at creation now groans with all of creation in anticipation of the redemption of all things (Romans 8:18-26).

The work of creation was and continues to be the work of all three members of the Trinity. Their roles are distinct, but they function in perfect harmony. The Father is the architect and source of all things; the Son is the model and content and the one through whom all things came into being (John 1:1); and the Spirit is the engineer or builder, the one who effects the vision of the triune God and brings it about. By the Spirit, the wind of God, out of darkness came light; out of chaos came order; out of formlessness came beauty; out of the void came the deep logic of the Earth located within our solar system and the galaxies that surround it.

As we read in Genesis 1, God declared—again and again—that it is *good*. The resulting creation reflects the perfect will of the Father and the image of the Son. In Genesis 1, we also see the connection between the Word ("God spoke") and the wind or breath of God: the Spirit and the Word in tandem bring about the deep goodness that is witnessed to in the opening chapter of Scripture. The Spirit, acting in perfect congruence with Father and Son, brings into being that which calls forth the praise of the psalmist:

> By the word of the Lord the heavens were made,
> and all their host by the breath of his mouth. (Psalm 33:6)

Few have witnessed to this as powerfully as the English poet Gerard Manley Hopkins, whose magisterial poem "God's Grandeur" opens with the line, "The world is charged with the grandeur of God," and concludes with these words:

> Oh, morning, at the brown brink eastward, springs—
> Because the Holy Ghost over the bent
> World broods with warm breast and with ah! bright wings.[2]

The Spirit is referenced here as the hovering bird or dove. The same Spirit who as a dove comes upon Jesus at his baptism is the Spirit who hovers over all things and brings them into being in all their beauty, glory, and majesty.

MATERIALITY INFUSED WITH THE BREATH OF GOD

By locating our understanding of the Holy Spirit within the broader vision of creation, we see the deep *physicality* of the Spirit's ministry. We recognize that embodiment and materiality are integral to the vision and purposes of God. The creation is tangible and concrete; we can affirm that physicality is good— indeed, *very* good.

---

[2]Gerard Manley Hopkins, "God's Grandeur," in *The Major Works* (Oxford: Oxford University Press, 1986), 128.

Two things come together when we do this. First, we see the materiality of creation, which in turn leads us to appreciate our own embodiment as human persons and the embodiment of our faith and Christian experience. It is not a biblical theology of the Spirit if we imply that the created order is less than good. It is also false to suggest that true spiritual worship is somehow disembodied or ethereal. The church throughout all of her history has been tempted to discount the physical. Regardless of the source, we need to call it out and insist that true spirituality is deeply physical; it is embodied. We need to witness to and celebrate the Spirit who at creation brought into being the earth in all of its beauty, in the incarnation brought about the fully embodied Christ Jesus, and at Pentecost brought into being the community that we speak of as the *body* of Christ. Again and again, the Spirit brings about the deeply and tangibly physical.

This is especially pertinent when it comes to countering the common assumption that if the Spirit is present and active, the normal, ordinary, and the routine is suspended. Many seem to almost celebrate the work of the Spirit precisely as that which bypasses the routine ways in which we function and worship. But when we anchor our understanding in the affinity between the Spirit and creation, and thus with embodiment, we appreciate that the Spirit works in the ordinary, in the routines and habits and disciplines of our daily lives, in those actions and ways of being that are very much in the body, of the earth, integral to the materiality of our lives and what it means to be created beings. We come to a fuller recognition that we are embodied souls. Our embodiment is not a problem but an inherent and beautiful reflection of the Spirit's presence and power in creation and in our lives.

One implication of this affirmation of our materiality is our appreciation for the sacramental life of the church—those deeply physical actions of baptism and the Lord's Supper—and other tangible ways by which we signal and appropriate the ministry of the Spirit in the life of the church, such as the laying on of hands or the anointing of the sick. Rather than minimizing or marginalizing these actions, we instead appreciate the Spirit is present to us specifically through these ordained means of grace. Just as the glory of God is revealed through the creation that came into being by the power of the Spirit, in like manner the Spirit is present to us and gracing us in that which we taste and touch.

But we need to go further. Yes, we can affirm the materiality of creation and the physicality of the Spirit's work of both creation and redemption. However, it is equally imperative that we see that materiality is only animated by the life-giving presence of the Spirit. Genesis 2:7 references the breath or wind of God as breathed into the first human person, reminding us that materiality, however good it is, requires the animation that comes with the Spirit's presence and grace to fulfill its identity as the creation. I will speak to this more fully when contrasting spirit and flesh, calling for our lives to be lived in radical dependence on the Spirit—saying that we are only alive when we live in the grace and power of God. But we start here: the breath or wind of God brings materiality, embodiment, to life.

And we also need to affirm that this is ongoing; it is continuous. We see this when we see the context of the verse from Psalm 104 quoted above. The reference to the Spirit is made within a broader affirmation of the immediacy of God to the creation, sustaining all that God has made:

These all look to you
    to give them their food in due season;
when you give to them, they gather it up;
    when you open your hand, they are filled with good things.
When you hide your face, they are dismayed;
    when you take away their breath, they die and return to their dust.
When you send forth your spirit, they are created;
    and you renew the face of the ground. (Psalm 104:27-30)

In Job also, we see the testimony of Elihu to the radical dependence of all creation on the immediacy of God's sustaining presence:

If he should take back his spirit to himself,
    and gather to himself his breath,
all flesh would perish together,
    and all mortals return to dust. (Job 34:14-15)

This can be seen as a parallel to our own breathing—in which we inhale, oxygen fills our lungs, and our bodies are infused with life. We die, physically, when we stop breathing. In like manner, the wind of God—the Spirit—is everywhere and always sustaining all of life, animating everything—every plant, every bird, every living thing.

We will consider further the relationship between Word and Spirit in a later chapter, but it merits mention now that this same principle—life through Spirit-inbreathing—applies to the way we engage the Scriptures. The words of 2 Timothy 3:16 are noteworthy, where the Scriptures are spoken of as "God-breathed" (NIV). The Scriptures are but letters—script on paper—apart from the animating power and grace of the Spirit—in the same way that a body is nothing but physicality apart from the infusion of divine breath. But further, the Scriptures are God-breathed and inspired not just when the prophets and apostles *wrote* the words of Scripture; they become life to us even now insofar as the Spirit informs and illumines us through our reading and preaching of the Scriptures. Scripture is only transformative in our lives through the animating grace of the Spirit. This applies to their original inspiration but, as noted above with respect to all creation and our own breathing, the presence of the Spirit is also ongoing when the Scriptures are read and proclaimed.

THE SPIRIT AS THE ONE BY WHICH THE CREATION IS RENEWED

In the Scriptures, there is a powerful contrast between Genesis 1 and Romans 8. In Genesis, the Spirit as Creator, with the Father and the Son, hovers over the void and the darkness, and out of darkness and void brings light and life. Then in Romans 8:18-27 we read that the whole of creation is groaning in anticipation of the day when the children of God will be revealed. In the meantime, the Spirit groans with us with sighs too deep for words.

Now, of course, we only appreciate this profound work of the Spirit in creation and redemption if we have some sense that indeed the salvation of God incorporates all that God has made. It is helpful to consider the work of the Spirit against the backdrop of the work of the ascended Christ, for they work in harmony and tandem. The Spirit is the one who fulfills what was accomplished in the ascension. Thus we read in Ephesians:

> God put this power to work in Christ when he raised him from the dead and seated him at his right hand in the heavenly places, far above all rule and authority and power and dominion, and above every name that is named, not only in this age but also in the age to come. And he has put all things under his feet and has made

him the head over all things for the church, which is his body, the
fullness of him who fills all in all. (Ephesians 1:20-23)

The work of the Spirit fulfills this cosmic vision of the ascended
Christ ruling over all things.

Recognizing this grand and thorough work of God in creation,
we then read Romans 8 through a different lens: we have the beginnings of an appreciation of the work of the Spirit who is attending the deep fragmentation of our world, its brokenness, with
a vision and capacity to bring healing to all that God has made.

On the one hand, we have the prior and essential work of the
Spirit who groans with the creation (Romans 8:26-27) but then
also actively tends to what needs to happen to make things well.
In the language of John 16:8-11, the Spirit is convicting, judging,
and challenging the old order, the fallen order, the deadly order,
pressing for and insisting on restoration and healing. In other
words, the Spirit does not leave things alone in their fragmentation and brokenness but actively challenges what is within us
and all that God has made that is not of God or undermines the
purposes of God.

The Spirit who is the means by which all things come into being
is the same Spirit who is now bent on the healing of creation. Our
own experience of the Spirit, individually and in the church, must
be known and experienced in light of this cosmic vision.

THE SCIENTIST AND THE ARTIST

It follows, then, that if this matters to the Spirit, it matters to us. If
we walk in the Spirit, we will embrace the call to tend to the created
order and attend to its renewal and restoration. We will take delight
in its beauty and appreciate how we are graced, by the Spirit, through
the natural order. But more, we will also be instruments of

healing—groaning with the Spirit when the environment is despoiled, repenting of how we have not adequately tended to its well-being, and changing our behavior and actively seeking to care for the garden in which we have been placed. We truly only walk in the Spirit when we respond to the Spirit's initiative to be the hands and feet of the Spirit in the restoration and healing of the creation. For Christian believers to be profoundly committed to environmental justice is not some secular agenda; it is rather that the Spirit is inviting and empowering them to do what the Spirit is doing.

While this is a call to all, it also is appropriate to highlight the work of those invited by the Spirit into the sciences and the arts. If what has been said thus far is true, there are profound implications for those who are called into the sciences, especially those who work in the earth sciences and those called to the study and care of flora and fauna. Could it be that they are agents of the Spirit as they work to tend the well-being of God's world? If so, would it not follow that we affirm and recognize that this work is at the heart of what the Spirit is up to and how we have been called to be the hands and feet of the Spirit in the world?

We must recognize that the scientists in our midst help all of us understand and appreciate the world as God has made it as a way to inspire our worship, much as the psalmist takes delight in the Creator by celebrating the creation. They are responding to the initiative of the Spirit when they address matters of environmental degradation or the extinction of species, and when they coach us in how to live with greater care and integrity as those who have been placed in this garden to care for it. The scientist in the field securing samples that signal noteworthy developments, and the scientist in the laboratory processing and interpreting these samples, are both doing the work of the Spirit.

We can also speak of artists as their colleagues in this essential work of witnessing to the beauty of the created order. Whether they are musicians, visual artists, poets, novelists, dancers, actors, quilters, weavers, or sculptors, we need to see the artists in our midst as those whose work calls forth the beauty of creation and, more, are the means by which we recognize and live in the wonder of the Spirit's presence. Thus our reflections on the Spirit must bring us to the witness in the Scriptures to Bezalel, who was filled with the Spirit and given unique intelligence and capacity in the arts—in every kind of craft, we read in Exodus 31:

> The LORD spoke to Moses: See, I have called by name Bezalel son of Uri son of Hur, of the tribe of Judah: and I have filled him with divine spirit, with ability, intelligence, and knowledge in every kind of craft, to devise artistic designs, to work in gold, silver, and bronze, in cutting stones for setting, and in carving wood, in every kind of craft. Moreover, I have appointed with him Oholiab son of Ahisamach, of the tribe of Dan; and I have given skill to all the skillful, so that they may make all that I have commanded you: [7] the tent of meeting, and the ark of the covenant, and the mercy seat that is on it, and all the furnishings of the tent, the table and its utensils, and the pure lampstand with all its utensils, and the altar of incense, and the altar of burnt offering with all its utensils, and the basin with its stand, and the finely worked vestments, the holy vestments for the priest Aaron and the vestments of his sons, for their service as priests, and the anointing oil and the fragrant incense for the holy place. They shall do just as I have commanded you. (Exodus 31:1-11)

While the primary reference here is to the liturgical arts—the way in which the arts accompany and foster worship—the call to Bezalel has implications for every aspect of the life, work, and witness of the church. As Hans Urs von Balthasar has stressed, beauty is indispensable to life; and, further, beauty is the means by which God is revealed to us and present to us.[3] Thus the artists in our midst are crucial gifts of the Spirit; they are *charismata*. Artists enable the church and the world to know the beauty, holiness, and love of the Creator. They witness to the presence and power of the Spirit; they are evangelists in speaking not merely to the healing of creation but also to appreciating the grace and power of the Spirit in creation. They do this not only through religious art, though that has its place; rather, they witness to the ineffable and the transcendent in all that they do. They call forth our best selves as we, in our work and relationships, witness to the grace of the Spirit.

Both the scientist and the artist would appreciate the twelfth-century witness of Hildegard of Bingen (1098–1179), canonized in 2012 by Benedict XVI. She was a theologian but also a mystic and a scientist, a musician and poet. Her work as a theologian was complemented and infused by her prayers and by her love of science and the arts. Hildegard reminds us that the scientists among us are attending to the deep work of the Spirit in creation, while artists call us to recognize the presence of the Spirit in our lives and in our world. Hildegard could well be the patron saint of both scientists and artists, but for all of us she points us to the witness of such texts as Psalm 104, with its remarkable ode to creation—sheer delight in all that God has made. This should, in turn, lead us to appreciate the scientists and artists in our midst, and appreciate and bless them in their work, seeing them to be vanguards of the Spirit. Her rich appreciation of the place of the

---

[3]See his *The Glory of the Lord: A Theological Aesthetics: Volume I: Seeing the Form* (San Francisco: Ignatius Press, 1982).

Spirit in creation comes through in her "O Fire of God," which picks up on two of the metaphors identified in the prelude—fire and living water:

> O Fire of God, the Comforter, O life of all that live,
> Holy art thou to quicken us, and holy, strength to give:
> To heal the broken-hearted ones, their sorest wounds to bind,
> O Spirit of all holiness, O Lover of mankind!
> O sweetest taste within the breast, O grace upon us poured,
> That saintly hearts may give again their perfume to the Lord.
> O purest fountain! We can see, clear mirrored in thy streams,
> That God brings home the wanderers, that God the lost redeems.[4]

TENDING THE GARDEN

Creation care is at the heart of what it means to walk in the Spirit. It cannot be politicized as though it is the agenda of a specific party or movement. Christians of all political stripes should be firm advocates for environmental justice, for practices that sustain the beauty and integrity of the creation and that tend the creation for its beauty and thus its witness to the Creator.

Thus, gardening may be a spiritual practice by which we live in intentional alignment with the Spirit. Tending the earth— gardening, along with the care of the animal world, including birding, husbandry, and sheepherding—grounds us in the stuff of creation and thus aligns our hearts more acutely with the Spirit, who is bringing about the renewal of all things.

The gardeners among us call us to walk in the Spirit by attending to what the Spirit has brought into being, that all of us might learn to care for the created order. As noted, creation care is not

---

[4]Translated from the Latin by R. F. Littledale.

something that for the Christian is a matter of some political platform. We must rise above the ideologies of particular political parties and insist that as Christians we will tend the garden. We will seek to foster sustainable ways of living and working that foster our stewardship of God's creation. We will discern how the Spirit is calling us to play our part in creation care because of what we believe about the Spirit and creation. Tending the creation is not merely a matter of attending to our own personal gardens; it is about tending the garden in which we as humanity have been placed, and the small plots of land we tend are microcosms of the garden that is the creation.

Those who walk in the Spirit will learn to tend the garden, the environment, individually and as a community. A powerful example of a Spirit-inspired engagement with the creation is planting trees. Yes, we reduce and recycle and wean ourselves off our proclivity to be consumers. But tree planting is an example of how we might go further and *restore* the garden. It is interesting to see how Orthodox Christians in Ethiopia have come to see themselves as stewards of forests.[5] Priests are leading a movement that has them planting trees around their churches; if you see a grove of trees in rural Ethiopia it must mean there is a church within the trees. Church planting and tree planting go hand in hand. The message for each congregation is reinforced by the proclamation that God's people are stewards of the earth, called to live responsibly within nature. Encouraged by this movement within the church and nonprofit organizations like Planting with Purpose, Ethiopia set a goal to plant four billion trees in the summer of 2019. This is work that is inspired by the Spirit and is

---

[5]Amir Aman Kiyaro, "The Churches in the Trees," *Christianity Today*, vol 63, no. 7 (Sept 2019): 54-58.

aligned with and in tune with the Spirit's work of renewing and restoring the created order.

When we come to the culmination of human history at the consummation of the reign of Christ, we will enter into the new city. Revelation 21 speaks of how God will dwell in this place, but more, that the "glory and honor of the nations" will be brought into the city. We will bring into the kingdom of God the best of the work of the scientists among us and those who, on our behalf, bring what we have cultivated—in food, wine, music, visual art, and dance. And we will celebrate the work of the scientists who have been prophets among us, coaching us and teaching us what it means to live with integrity in God's creation as a foretaste of the day when all will be made well.

Thus, it should be evident—in the upcoming reflections on our experience of the Spirit and the church as the fellowship of the Spirit—that the only Spirit we know is the Spirit by whom all things have come into being and by whom all things are being renewed to the greater glory of Christ. It is this Spirit whom we long to know. This is the Spirit who brought all things into being, and who groans with us for the renewal of all things, and that is the focus of our longings when we say, "Welcome, Holy Spirit."

CHAPTER FOUR

THE SPIRIT AND
CHRISTIAN INITIATION

*T*HE NEW TESTAMENT and the whole of the Christian intellectual and spiritual tradition agree that the Christian life can only be lived through the empowering grace of the Holy Spirit. The journey of Christian faith is one where the Christian and the church learn to live in dependence on the Spirit—that is, to "live by the Spirit" (Galatians 5:16).

But what does this mean for our *initiation* into the Christian faith and the life of the church? How is it that this journey in the Spirit *begins*? Is it is appropriate to speak of the reception of the Spirit as something *integral* to the process of becoming a believer, or is it a *distinct* experience that comes at a later point in the Christian journey? On this question and related questions, there is much diversity of opinion and practice. Indeed, as a rule, there are two different and, seemingly, opposing views—both of which merit our consideration. Before I consider the two views on this matter, it is important to acknowledge that I am assuming that the Christian life is life in community, in fellowship with the church. We are initiated into life in the Spirit through the reception of the gift of the Spirit, and this presumes incorporation into Christian community. The only Spirit we know is the Spirit that is given to the church, and we are only in fellowship with the Spirit if we are in communion with the community of faith. It is from this basic assumption that I will speak to the experience of the individual Christian and consider what it means to be initiated into life in the Spirit.

CONVERSION, INITIATION, AND
THE GIFT OF THE SPIRIT: TWO VIEWS

View 1. In the first view, conversion is one thing and the reception of the gift of the Spirit is another. They are two distinct experiences. I grew up within the Holiness-Pentecostal tradition, which adopts this view. When I was ordained for pastoral office within my denomination, I had to fill out a form in which I had to identify two dates. First, I needed to specify the date when I became a Christian. It was assumed that conversion was punctiliar; it was, to use the language of my revivalist upbringing, a "decision." It took place in a single event in which you believed in Christ; you accepted that Christ was and is Savior and Lord; you repented of your former way of life. All of that could occur on one day, often during what we used to speak of as an "altar call." The preacher gave the invitation to become a Christian believer and, if you felt so inclined, you went forward and prayed "the sinner's prayer," often with the assistance of others. The experience was datable: you could identify the time and the place when this happened. On one day you were not a Christian; the next day, you were a follower of Jesus. Any reference to the Spirit in all of this was largely that it was the Spirit who was drawing me and others and convicting us of sin and of our need for Christ.

But to be ordained, not only did I need to specify the date when I was converted, I also needed to identify the date when I was "filled with the Spirit." The assumption was that this second date came later, sometimes much later. Many would speak of a struggle to live the Christian life that led them to realize that apart from the Spirit their situation was hopeless—they were struggling to find "victory over sin" and lacking a deep and abiding joy. There would typically be a gathering where the speaker would invite one and all to know the sanctified life that came through the gift of the Spirit. As with conversion, this was punctiliar: you knew when it happened; you could date the time and identify the place where you were "filled with the Spirit." In my faith community, the experience of the Spirit was spoken of as both a crisis (that is, punctiliar) and progressive.[1] The assumption, of course, was that you did not have the progressive experience unless you had had the crisis: the moment of receiving this gift.

There are many variations on this way of speaking about the ministry of the Spirit, but the fundamental perspective is that the journey to faith and knowing the grace of the Spirit is a two-stage process. The gift of the Spirit is not only distinct from conversion, but also something that came later. Many assumed that this experience of receiving the Spirit included a notable manifestation—whether it was tongue-speaking, a deeply moving or heightened emotional experience, or some physical manifestation such that there was no doubt that one had received the "gift."

This assumption that water baptism and Spirit baptism are distinct and thus potentially separated in time was and in many

---

[1] Article 7 of the doctrinal statement of the Christian and Missionary Alliance reads: "It is the will of God that each believer should be filled with the Holy Spirit and be sanctified wholly, being separated from sin and the world and fully dedicated to the will of God, thereby receiving power for holy living and effective service. This is both a crisis and a progressive experience wrought in the life of the believer subsequent to conversion." http:// www.norwinalliance.org/statement-of-faith.php. This is the statement of faith of the Christian and Missionary Alliance in the United States, and was—it has since been revised—the statement of the Christian and Missionary Alliance in Canada when I was ordained to pastoral ministry.

respects continues to be the assumption within the Roman Catholic Church in its distinction between water baptism—typically of a newborn infant—and confirmation, when the grace of the Spirit is imparted to the now-ready-for-adulthood Christian through the formal blessing of the bishop. In the Eastern church, chrismation typically comes immediately after and with the baptism of the infant. In Protestant denominations that practice infant baptism, confirmation is typically more of an affirmation of faith—the emerging adult accepting the promise that was made on his or her behalf at their baptism. But the Catholic perspective links confirmation to "chrismation": that is, the anointing that signifies the granting of the gift of the Spirit. The *Catechism of the Catholic Church* puts it this way: "It is evident from its celebration that the effect of the sacrament of Confirmation is the special outpouring of the Holy Spirit as once granted to the apostles on the day of Pentecost."[2]

View 2. However, many Christians would insist that baptism and the reception of the Spirit are not separate because the reception of the gift of the Spirit is integral to Christian conversion and is essentially automatic: if you became a Christian, you have received this gift. There is no need for a conscious appropriation of a particular experience of the Spirit. Indeed, some would contend that making such a request essentially discounts the meaning of conversion and faith in Christ. They would insist that you cannot separate Christ and the Spirit; you cannot have Christ except by and in the Spirit. Therefore, you simply need to trust that in affirming that Christ Jesus is Lord, the gift of the Holy Spirit is given to you. You merely need to press on and learn to walk in the grace of the Spirit and increasingly learn to depend on the Spirit.

---

[2]Catholic Church, *Catechism of the Catholic Church*, 2nd ed. (Vatican City: Libreria Editrice Vaticana, 1997), par. 1302.

Those of this perspective would agree that the Christian life must be lived in the fullness of the Spirit and in radical dependence on the grace of the Spirit. But they would see no need for a dramatic or decisive "filling" or "baptism" of the Spirit. They might see this as a bit of a distraction; instead, we all need to simply learn to live in and walk in the Spirit. And they are likely to take some offense when their friends and neighbors do not think they truly live in the grace of the Spirit because they have not had a definitive experience that they would attribute to the Spirit.

Thus we have these two views, seemingly polar opposites. As often as not in our conversations, they are portrayed as reflecting two different perspectives on what it means to become a Christian and what it means to be filled with the Spirit. And yet, might there be something worth considering with both of these perspectives? Might there also be a limitation or problem with each? Could there be a way forward that actually draws on the wisdom of both views?

This might also mean that we rethink how we approach the practice of water baptism. In both views, it is not uncommon for little if any reference to be made to the Spirit at baptism. For the first view, the gift of the Spirit will come later—in due time or at one's confirmation. For the second view, the work of the Spirit is more understated, and thus assumed. I wonder if both perspectives need a gentle correction that leads us to greater intentionality—both in our speaking but also our actions—when it comes to the significance of the Spirit in the journey to faith and our practices of Christian initiation.

THE GIFT OF THE SPIRIT AND CHRISTIAN INITIATION

The gift of the Holy Spirit as integral to initiation. First, we need to agree with the second view that the gift of the Spirit is *integral* to Christian faith—so essential that we simply cannot speak of conversion and Christian initiation without reference to the gift of the Spirit. For some in the book of Acts the reception of the gift of the Spirit seemed, if not actually was, a distinct experience, and we can explore those narratives and plumb their significance. But our *primary* point of reference is that the gift is by its very nature integral to Christian identity and experience. The apostle Paul presumes this: the Galatians received the gift of the Spirit because they believed (Galatians 3:1-3). He was distressed because they seemingly were attempting to live the Christian life as though they had not received this gift, the Spirit by which they could live the Christian life. They had received the Spirit, and they were charged to live their Christian lives accordingly.

We cannot separate our experience of Christ from this gift; even if they are distinct, surely the baptism of the Spirit is an essential complement to water baptism. We cannot sustain a perspective wherein the grace and power of the Spirit is "subsequent" to our encounter with and reception of Christ in our lives. We cannot have Christ and not the Spirit; we cannot separate these two persons of the Trinity. We cannot suggest that in receiving Christ we have a good thing but that we need to go further and receive the gift of the Spirit, as though somehow we need more than what we have in Christ. Yes, we are eager to encourage Christian believers to lean into and depend even more on the ministry of the Spirit, but we do not do this by suggesting that Christ is not sufficient. We are always drawn by the Spirit—both in coming to faith and then in growing in faith—into greater union with Christ.

Consider the following references in Scripture and what they mean for our understanding of the gift of the Spirit at Christian initiation—using in particular the Gospel of John and the book of Acts. Foundationally, we have the promise of John 1:32 that the Messiah who is to come will baptize not merely with water, but with the Holy Spirit. Then, on the day of Pentecost, those present observed that something powerful and transformative had happened in the lives of Peter and the others. They wondered what this meant, and they too wanted this gift. In response, Peter preached a sermon on the ascension of Christ Jesus and made reference to the promise of Joel that the Spirit would come and be poured out on all humanity. When those present asked what they should do, Peter gave them the paradigmatic response: "Repent and be baptized . . . so that your sins may be forgiven; and you will receive the gift of the Holy Spirit." Peter then assures them that if indeed they repent and are baptized, they will receive the gift of the Spirit (Acts 2:38).

The logic would be that the gift of the Spirit comes after the rite of water baptism. However, when later the apostle Peter is preaching in the home of Cornelius, there is a sudden movement of the Spirit and the whole household is baptized with this gift— which, we read, was a surprise to Peter and the Jewish leaders who had come with him to the home of Cornelius. They had not anticipated that non-Jews would also receive the Spirit. But when it happened, Peter knew what he needed to do: "Can anyone withhold the water for baptizing these people who have received the Holy Spirit just as we have?" (Acts 10:47). We then read they were then promptly baptized in the name of Jesus Christ (Acts 10:48).

There are two things to note here. First, the sequence did not reflect the simple statement of Acts 2:38, likely because they did not yet fully appreciate that the Gentile world would receive the Spirit without first becoming Jews. And yet, second, both happened, suggesting that the two were distinct and inseparable. The two—water baptism and the gift of the Spirit—were twinned. They are distinct, but both are needed; both are necessary to Christian initiation. Receiving the gift of the Spirit does not mean that one does not need to submit to water baptism, and water baptism is necessarily complemented by the reception of the Spirit.

This seems to reflect the language and intent of John 3 when Jesus speaks to Nicodemus of the need for a new birth—the need for regeneration—and states bluntly: "No one can enter the kingdom of God without being born of water and Spirit" (v. 5). For those of the Eastern Orthodox Church, this remarkable affirmation speaks of the interplay between water baptism and the gift of the Spirit: they are distinct, though inseparable. And in many respects this is what lies behind the conviction of the Eastern church that the two should not—better, *cannot*—be separated. In the epistle to Titus they are easily and naturally linked when we read: "But when the goodness and loving kindness of God our Savior appeared, he saved us, not because of any works of righteousness that we had done, but according to his mercy, through the water of rebirth and renewal by the Holy Spirit. This Spirit he poured out on us richly through Jesus Christ our Savior" (Titus 3:4-6).

The Spirit who is given to us through Christ accompanies "the water of rebirth." Some in the evangelical tradition may struggle with the way in which the Titus reference makes a close connection between "[God] saved us" and "the water of rebirth." But the straightforward reading assumes that our faith is physical and that our initiation, much like we see in Acts 2:38, is not merely interior—it is also *exterior*, that is, in the body. The physical act of baptism is accompanied by the renewing work of the Spirit.

Then, at the end of the Gospel of John, Jesus comes to the encounter with his disciples, after the cross and resurrection, in anticipation of his ascension. There we read: "Jesus said to them again, 'Peace be with you. As the Father has sent me, so I send you.' When he had said this, he breathed on them and said to them, 'Receive the Holy Spirit'" (John 20:21-22). Some speak of this as the "Johannine Pentecost"—John's version of what Luke describes in Acts 2. But John's Gospel has already made it clear that the gift of the Spirit is intimately linked to the ascension. In John 14, Jesus makes the point that it is the Father who will send the Spirit even as Jesus is going to the Father (John 14:16), and then in John 16 he declares that the coming of the Spirit depends on his going—that is, that the Spirit will only come as Jesus returns to the Father (John 16:7). Then he adds, "If I go, I will send him to you." Here, it is Jesus that is sending. Clearly, it is both the Father and the Son— that is, the Father sends in response to the request of the Son and through the Son. But the main point is that Pentecost, as we speak of it, is post-ascension.

Yet this is a treasured text of Scripture—this powerful commission and the declaration that the peace of Christ will be with his disciples. Of the many ways in which the text can be read, the one that seems to make the most sense—recognizing that John's Gospel was written after the book of Acts—is that this is the reminder and assurance as we read John that there is no other way to live as a disciple of Jesus except in the power of the Spirit. Thus we might speak of this as a statement of anticipation: Jesus breathes on his disciples and declares that the Spirit is given to them, and indeed, the full experience of Pentecost comes soon after. The lives of the disciples would include and rightly assume this gift. As Jesus promised in John 16, in his going he is leaving them another, the Advocate. To be a follower of Christ is to be graced by the gift of the Spirit.

Rethinking the character of conversion. However, what do we make of those who seem to have had a kind of two-stage initiation to faith? What does it mean that their baptism had little if any reference to the Spirit, and that they had a later experience of the Spirit that seemed to be not linked to their baptism or their initial steps as Christians? As noted, for some—such as the heirs to the Holiness-Pentecostal tradition—this delayed experience of knowing the grace of the Spirit is actually part of their theological formulations—that is, their faith statements.

But there might be a way to bring these two views together if we acknowledge that the conversion process itself is complex. We would begin by affirming that the gift of the Spirit is integral to Christian conversion and is an essential complement to the rite of water baptism. But we would lean into the wisdom of the Holiness-Pentecostal perspective precisely at this point: that the experience of coming to faith is complex. This is particularly the case in a post-Christian and secular society, in which conversion is both a complex experience and an *extended* experience—a journey to faith with many elements that are not all appropriated in a nice, neat package. Each journey will be different. For some it might transpire more quickly than for others, but as a rule, conversion will be an extended and a staged process.

In other words, every coming to faith in Christ needs to include the reception of the gift of the Spirit as something integral to what it means to becoming a Christian. But this experience cannot be choreographed by the church or by the individual who is coming to faith. It might be the case that for some the journey to faith will be in fits and starts, at some point will include water baptism, but the full experience of the grace of the Spirit will come not immediately but in due time. In other cases, the gift of the Spirit—as with Cornelius—might come *before* one is water baptized. We could make the case that the gift of the Spirit is essential to Christian initiation but we do not try to choreograph it. Instead, we *witness* to it and then let the Spirit do what only the Spirit can do, in the grace and timing of the Spirit. This means the existential experience of the gift of the Spirit, while witnessed to at baptism, may actually come later.

At water baptism, we can and should ask for the gift of the Spirit to come upon a new Christian believer. We witness to the gift of the Spirit; we celebrate the gift of the Spirit. It may be *experientially* separate from water baptism, but theologically we must view them as part of a whole. And we must speak of them as a whole, as integral to each other. In coming to faith in Christ, we move toward an intentional expectation of and receptivity to the gift of the Spirit. But we do this without forcing the issue or presuming that we can manage how, when, and in what circumstances the Spirit will come to this person as part of their journey to faith.

The importance of a rite of Spirit-initiation. This means we speak of the gift of the Spirit as integral to the journey to faith; the reception of this gift is a vital element in Christian initiation. It follows that we would speak about this when we outline a theological vision for conversion, and that we would witness to the gift of the Spirit as part of the rites of Christian initiation. Logically, this would happen on the occasion of a person's baptism.

For my purposes, I am going to speak to the practice within my own tradition, where the people being baptized are either emerging adults appropriating the faith of their heritage or people who are entirely new to the faith—what is typically spoken of as water baptism by immersion. Those who practice infant baptism can take what is offered here and consider the implications for their own circumstances.

Regarding adults who are baptized on the basis of their own confession of faith, we must consider both what we say (what is spoken as part of the rite of baptism) and what we do (how we might symbolize or ritualize this gift). First, the rite of water baptism must include intentional reference to the Holy Spirit. Baptism is a water rite, but it is more than that. It is also a rite wherein we declare that this person who is coming to faith is entering into a journey where they will live not self-sufficient lives but lives of intentional dependence on the Spirit. And so, we *talk* about the Spirit. We affirm that it is by the gift of the Spirit that this person has come to this stage in their journey of faith; we know that the Spirit and the Spirit alone is the one who brought this about—through the words and witness of many, no doubt, but all with the recognition that the Spirit did what only the Spirit can do. Then also, we declare that no one lives the Christian life unless they receive grace from on high—the gift of the Spirit. It is irresponsible to baptize a person and not also grant them the essential resources to live the life into which they are being baptized. And so, as part of the baptism it only makes sense that we would also ask that the gift of the Spirit come upon this new child of God and grace them for the life and work to which they are being called as a disciple of Christ Jesus.

Second, while we witness to the Spirit at baptism, why not go further and have a Spirit-rite that signals *tangibly* the grace and power of the Spirit as an essential counterpart to the water rite? Here, the wisdom of our Christian heritage gives us a way forward that would embody this gift in the life of the newly minted Christian—visible practices that would accompany the spoken word and the request for the gift of the Spirit. First is the laying on of hands. We read that the apostle Paul's coming to faith in Christ included the powerful encounter with Ananias after he had been blinded by the bright light:

> So Ananias went and entered the house. He laid his hands on Saul and said, "Brother Saul, the Lord Jesus, who appeared to you on your way here, has sent me so that you may regain your sight and be filled with the Holy Spirit." And immediately something like scales fell from his eyes, and his sight was restored. Then he got up and was baptized, and after taking some food, he regained his strength. (Acts 9:17-19)

The laying on of hands signals identification by the church with the new Christian; the experience of coming to faith is not solitary but one where you are accompanied by others, notably those who are leaders in the community of faith.

Second is the oil of anointing. The links between the Spirit and the anointing oil are numerous in Scripture, including the intriguing reference in 1 John 2 that speaks of the Father and the Son and also the anointing of the Holy One (1 John 2:20, 27). The idea here is that the presence and power of the Spirit in the life of the newly baptized is represented through anointing. Whether it is the sign of the cross on the forehead or the bathing of the head in oil, it is a "chrismation," the formal rite signaling the Spirit's anointing.

In using the language of "chrismation," I am borrowing from the Eastern tradition, but there is no reason why this should be a particularly Eastern or Orthodox way of speaking of the Spirit and initiation. It is an apt word to speak of the Spirit-rite that can and, I am suggesting, *should* accompany baptism.

In so doing, we would be following ancient precedent—going all the way back to the early church catechumenate established by Ambrose of Milan and given full expression by Augustine the bishop of Hippo. For Ambrose and Augustine, the oil of anointing was an integral element of the process of Christian initiation. There is wisdom from the pre-Christendom church for the church in a post-Christian and secular age.[3]

Third is the breath of God. In some cases, the presiding minister lays hands on the baptized one, anoints with oil, and then breathes on them, pronounces their name, and calls them to receive the gift of the Spirit, echoing the experience of the first disciples as described in John 20:21-22.

The main point in all of this is that the reception of the gift of the Spirit is indispensable to faith. We need to declare this—speak to it as part of the process by which a person is welcomed into and initiated into life in Christ—but we also need to ritualize it. We should signify that we are asking for the gift of the Spirit for this our new sister and brother in the faith, and represent this through the laying on of hands, the oil of anointing, and by breathing on them and calling them to receive this gift into their hearts and minds.

But this benchmark experience, linked to baptism, is not one where either the one who is baptized or the presiding minister

---

[3]This is indeed the assumption behind the "Rite for the Christian Initiation of Adults," the process by which those who are initiated into the Catholic Church are brought along a journey to faith. It is the standard practice that those who are baptized—as often as not by aspersion, with a threefold baptism in the name of the Father, the Son, and the Spirit—are then also, using Catholic nomenclature, confirmed with the oil of anointing.

who presides over the baptism has control of the Spirit or can choreograph or manage the Spirit. Thus it is most helpful to speak of how in baptism and chrismation we signal the gift of the Spirit. In word and deed, we witness to this gift and ask for it. At that point, and moving forward, we trust that this person is and will be living in the Spirit. We do not need to ask and ask again, hoping for something dramatic or emotionally heightened to happen in their lives. Rather, they can now live in this realty and learn to depend on the Spirit and walk in the Spirit.

Does this person, this new Christian, have the Spirit? Yes, of course, and there may well be a benchmark moment in their journey—it may have come earlier or it may come later. The rite of chrismation is not causal. We do not make this gift happen. At the baptism, we *witness* to the gift; we do not manage the gift. Some may have a significant and emotionally intense experience of the Spirit at their baptism. For others, it may well be a quieter grace that they receive. The main point is that we have asked for this gift and witnessed to it, and now the new Christian can move forward and learn what it means to live in the Spirit.

IMPLICATIONS FOR EVANGELISM AND CATECHESIS

In all of these considerations, we should speak more extensively and teach more comprehensively about the Spirit as integral to the journey to faith. Yes, we must teach what it means to walk in the Spirit as we mature in the faith, and I will come to this in the next chapter. However, I am proposing that we teach about this as part of the process of *coming to faith* in Christ. The process of evangelism and catechesis—that is, the instruction that leads to baptism or informs the movement into an adult faith, following confirmation or the rites by which the faith spoken at one's birth is now your own faith—needs to unapologetically use language that references the Spirit.

At the least, this involves two things. First, provide a theological vision for the ministry of the Holy Spirit. Those coming into the Christian faith need to come to their rites of initiation with a basic pneumatology—at the least a simple appreciation of the triunity of God and an affirmation that, as they come to faith and mature in faith, they will learn what it is to recognize the inner witness of the Spirit (Romans 8:16) and learn to walk in the Spirit.[4]

Second, catechesis is not just about getting beliefs right, confirming doctrines, affirming the right Christian principles. It is not merely about intellectual assent to the truths of the Christian faith. As one moves into the faith and toward initiation into Christian community, it is essential that we attend to the disposition of the heart. If the imperative is that we know—in our hearts—the love of Christ (Romans 5:5), the love that surpasses knowledge (Ephesians 3:19), the love that is twinned in Ephesians 3 with the power of the Holy Spirit by which we are strengthened in our inner beings even as Christ dwells in our hearts by faith (Ephesians 3:16-17), then we need to attend to matters of the heart. We need to cultivate the capacity to be open, ready, and willing to receive the gift of the Spirit—to know in the depths of our beings that we are loved, to be responsive to the call and convicting ministry of the Spirit (see Psalm 139:23 and its prayer, "Search me, O God, and know my heart"), and to be willing to have God's very self dwell within us so that we no longer are autonomous but living in the freedom of a new identity and orientation as children of God.

---

[4]This book is written with this very idea in mind: to offer to those coming to faith a way of understanding and responding to the gift of Pentecost and then learning, in Christian community, to both receive this gift and then mature in Christian faith through the gracious work of the Spirit in our lives.

The Spirit is a gift that is given to those who are willing to *receive* the gift. A. W. Tozer, in his little book *How to Be Filled with the Holy Spirit*, makes this point effectively: it all comes down to *receptivity*.[5] Are we willing and emotionally able and disposed to lift up our hearts and be radically attentive to the presence of the Spirit within us? Christian catechesis and initiation needs to include, of course, an orientation to the Christian belief system and worldview, but this transition into the faith needs to also include the cultivation of this receptivity—learning how to open heart and mind to the work of the Spirit.

In all of this, we should recognize that it is not that the Spirit is waiting in the wings for us to affirm the work of Christ and ask to be filled with the Spirit. The Spirit is powerfully present to the world and to our lives before we are initiated into the faith. We could not come to faith apart from the gracious work of the Spirit calling, nudging, prompting, convicting, and illuminating head and heart.

But if the Spirit is present to us throughout the journey to faith, what changes with the reception of the gift of the Spirit? It is important to stress that nothing is gained by overstating what happens in the reception of the gift. The journey of faith is a long obedience, a pilgrimage to a distant city. Transformation is a slow and incremental process, as I will stress in the upcoming chapter. But then, what can we count on? What will be the evidence that we have, indeed, begun the journey well?

First, this is the benchmark occasion of our lives. It is foundational, and from now on is an important reference point as we journey in the faith. To use Roman Catholic language, the presence of the Spirit has been "confirmed" in us.

---

[5]A. W. Tozer, *How to Be Filled with the Holy Spirit* (Harrisburg, PA: Christian Publications, Inc., 1960).

And second, we have now accepted, or perhaps better, *yielded* with a definitive "yes" to the work of the Spirit. Now we know, with depth of conviction, that we are children of God (Galatians 4:6-7)— no longer slaves but children who cry out "Abba, Father" as the Spirit witnesses with our spirit that this is our true identity (Romans 8:16). This is foundational: we can only grow and mature in our faith to the degree that we have some level of confidence that indeed the Father's love in Christ has been poured into our hearts (Romans 5:5). We are children of God. This is our identity and the posture of our hearts. Thus the book of Ephesians links the power of the Spirit and the love of God in the powerful prayer and benediction that reads:

> I pray that, according to the riches of his glory, he may grant that you may be strengthened in your inner being with power through his Spirit, and that Christ may dwell in your hearts through faith, as you are being rooted and grounded in love. I pray that you may have the power to comprehend, with all the saints, what is the breadth and length and height and depth, and to know the love of Christ that surpasses knowledge, so that you may be filled with all the fullness of God. (Ephesians 3:16-19)

Many of us have grown up in Christian communities that assume we know that Jesus loves us "because the Bible tells us so." The testimony of Scripture is important, of course. But the knowledge of the love of God in our hearts is the fruit of the work of the Holy Spirit—that is, as witnessed to by Scripture, the love of God is "poured into our hearts through the Holy Spirit" (Romans 5:5).

The intimate knowledge of the love of God and the empowering presence of the Spirit are linked. The journey of faith toward maturity in Christ presumes this foundational experience: the gift of the Spirit and the *affective* awareness of the love of God and the confidence that we are children of God. It is therefore with eager minds and open hearts that we say, "Welcome, Holy Spirit."

HOLY SPIRIT EXPERIENCES

As we make the transition from beginning well in the Spirit, and the reception of the gift of the Spirit, to the journey to maturity in Christ as we learn to walk in the Spirit—which will be considered in the upcoming chapter—we must wrestle with a matter of noteworthy concern. In some circles, it is common to assume that the only real evidence of the Spirit, the only evidence that is truly transformative, is what is experienced in the dramatic moment—an event in our lives that is marked by the emotional high, an overwhelming sensory awareness of the presence and power of the Spirit. There are those who assume that the true indicator of religious leadership is that one has had such dramatic experiences, continues to have them, and then can in turn call forth the same in others.

Gatherings in these communities—not only Sunday worship, but conferences and assemblies—can be all about seeking a heightened emotional encounter with the Spirit, asking for a fresh visitation of the Spirit that will be evident in dramatic manifestations. There are venues that specialize in delivering an experience of a "manifest presence." Christians seek out these opportunities to step away from the humdrum of their lives to experience something that would be transformative for them.

The desire for this kind of experience comes from sincerely wanting to know the grace of God and to live in the power of the

Spirit. In itself, this is an appropriate desire—for oneself and for those one is called to serve. Yet we need to ask if this is truly the mark of authentic religious leadership, and if anything is gained by a continual appeal to these heightened experiences. Does this really foster the transformation and maturity in Christ that we seek? Might this kind of agenda actually be a distraction from the work of God? Might it perhaps miss the point of how the Spirit works? Might it unwittingly foster a kind of infantilization, undermining the deep work of the Spirit in our lives and in the church?

In his commentary on 2 Corinthians, Scott J. Hafemann suggests that this inclination is not new to our day, but is something the apostle Paul faced with the Corinthian congregation—and that therefore there might be guidance for us in this epistle for our response to similar phenomena in our day. As Hafemann notes, it is clear from 2 Corinthians 12 that Paul has had some kind of rapturous experience, yet it is telling that the apostle did not appeal to this or any experience to authenticate his ministry. He did not claim that his ministry was "anointed" because of this kind of rapturous experience. Rather, he chose to emphasize that he suffered for the gospel and that he could boast in the grace and power of Christ in the midst of his weakness (2 Corinthians 12:9).[1] This is what he appeals to so that he could legitimize his calling. Paul did not want to talk about his own dramatic experience of the Spirit. He wanted to talk about grace in weakness and hardship.

Hafemann observes that the pursuit of a "Holy Spirit experience" discounts the ordinary and assumes that only the unusual will do. This creates the problem of seeking more ecstasy over time, and this pursuit simply cannot deliver. Furthermore, it results not

---

[1] Scott J. Hafemann, *2 Corinthians*, NIV Application Commentary (Grand Rapids, MI: Zondervan, 2000), 474.

in maturity in Christ, but in "spiritual emptiness."[2] We keep going back to the well, hoping for a rapturous experience, and it is like an addiction: we want it more and more. Some end up being spectators, or—as George Gardiner puts it—they act the part. Or worse, they quit and assume that something is wrong with them because they are not having the same experience as the person standing next to them.[3]

This is a misguided search. Our deep longing must be to know Christ and grow in our capacity for faith, hope, and love. It is not all about an inspiring speaker. It is not about an experience, however overwhelming; it is not about heightened emotion, which in the end might actually be a distraction. We might have such experiences, but they cannot be choreographed. When we try, it only creates the illusion of the presence of the Spirit. Our deep longing is for Christ, not some experience; it is not about the experiential "high."

This pursuit can so easily draw our attention away from what needs to be our focus: the risen and ascended Christ. Thus we are distracted from the deep and transformative work of the Spirit that is found in the habituated and ordinary practices of the Christian life, which we will discuss in the next chapter.

---

[2]Hafemann, *2 Corinthians,* 475, quoting Arturo G. Azurdia, *Spirit Empowered Preaching: The Vitality of the Holy Spirit in Preaching* (Geanies House, Fearn, Rosshire, Great Britain: Christian Focus Publications, 1998), 49.

[3]Hafemann, *2 Corinthians,* 475, referencing Gardiner as quoted by Azurdia, *Spirit Empowered Preaching,* 49.

CHAPTER FIVE

THE SPIRIT AND TRANSFORMATION

From Beginnings to Maturity in Christ

WHEN WE CONSIDER the ministry of the Holy Spirit in a Christian believer, we need to talk about three things. First, as in chapter 4, we reflect on what it means to receive the gift of the Spirit as a dimension of Christian initiation. Second, we also need to have clarity about the goal of the Christian life—that is, to what end is the Spirit at work in our lives? And then, third, we need to consider the *means* by which the Spirit works to bring us to maturity in Christ. These are the beginning, the destination, and the means by which we come to this destination. The primary focus of this chapter will be on how the Spirit fulfills within us this ideal of human flourishing. But first, we need to look at the goal of the Christian life, to then set the stage for a consideration of the transforming work of the Spirit.

MATURITY IN CHRIST

Whether we have language for it or not, everyone longs to be complete—to fulfill the purpose for which we were created. In the same way that a child longs to grow up into adulthood and a person who is unwell physically or emotionally longs for healing and wholeness, there is within each of us a yearning to achieve our human capacity and potential—to become, one might say, the kind of person we were created to be.

The good news is that we have the capacity to be all that God created us to be through the gracious and sanctifying work of the Spirit. The Spirit is given such that we can know the transforming grace of God by which we are made whole and fulfill the purpose for which we were created.

There are several metaphors in Scripture for the Christian life and the work of the Spirit in our lives. There is the powerful image of sickness and health: we are sin-sick souls and the Spirit is the means by which we know healing and wholeness. There is also the metaphor of the journey: the Christian is on a pilgrimage to a desired destination, following Christ and guided by the Spirit to the "heavenly city." Then there is the powerful image of infancy and maturity. A new Christian is an infant in the faith and is called to move from infancy toward what it means to be mature—an adult faith. Thus 1 Peter 2:2 and the following verses speak of infants who mature as they are fed by the word, and Colossians 2:6-7 speaks of how, now that we have received Christ Jesus as Lord, we grow up, rooted in Christ, but moving toward the very maturity that Paul speaks of in the closing verses of Colossians 1 as our destiny.

One of the great dangers in the church is what we might call the propensity toward a kind of infantilization, or what Timothy Bergler calls "juvenilization."[1] Rather than cultivating genuine spiritual growth toward maturity—and adult faith—we foster instead a contentment with an adolescent faith, fed by entertaining

---

[1]Timothy E. Bergler, *The Juvenilization of American Christianity* (Grand Rapids, MI: Eerdmans, 2012).

public speaking or approaches to shared worship that do not call us to depth and breadth in our experience of God.

Whatever the shape of our congregational life or worship, the Spirit's agenda is surely one of nudging, pressing, calling, and animating us toward maturity. If we are walking in the Spirit, we will sense this constant movement in our hearts and lives toward an adult faith. We receive the gift of the Spirit at Christian initiation; now we learn to walk in the Spirit, pray in the Spirit, and respond to the calling and movement of the Spirit in our lives and in our communities that leads us and empowers us on this journey.

We need to affirm again and again something that is basic to the life and witness of the church: that spiritual growth toward maturity is a requirement and expectation; it is an integral part of what it means to be a Christian believer. Indeed, I will be speaking to this in an upcoming chapter as a high priority for what it means to be the church. But for now, in this context, I am going to speak about the individual Christian who, while in fellowship and in mutual dependence within Christian community, is called to move from infancy to maturity, from beginnings to the full measure of the human vocation.

The goal of the Christian can be delineated in different ways, but it all comes down to this: we are called to be mature in Christ Jesus. The apostle Paul states this pointedly in a number of places, including Ephesians, where the call is that we would all grow up to him who is our head, Christ Jesus. That is, the apostle longs for his readers to no longer be tossed back and forth as children but grow to maturity, which is described as "the measure of the full stature of Christ" (Ephesians 4:13-14). Then, when we turn to Colossians 1:27-30 and 2:6-7, here too we see that the vision of the

Christian life is radically christocentric: Christ in you the hope of glory (Colossians 1:27). The work of the apostle is to present each one mature in Christ (Colossians 1:28). Having received Christ Jesus as Lord, they are then to be rooted and established in him (Colossians 2:7). Our deep longing and aspiration is to know, love, and serve Christ. It is thus the intent of the Spirit that Christ would be formed within us (Galatians 4:19). Beyond this, it is helpful, not apart from but *in Christ*, to speak of four aspects of Christian maturity—four dimensions of what it means to fulfill our identity and purpose as Christian believers.[2]

To be mature in Christ is to become increasingly wise: to move from ignorance and foolishness to knowledge and understanding that finds ultimate expression in wisdom. To be mature in Christ is to be a wise person. This includes, as we see from the book of Proverbs, moral intelligence: integrity of speech, sexuality, and finances. And it is the fruit of teaching; we attend to wise teachers so that we grow in wisdom.

Second, to be mature in Christ is to know what it means to love others as we have been loved, and then in turn to live in love with and for others. Just as the church is a teaching-learning community that grows in wisdom, it is also a school of love where we learn what it means to be hospitable to one another, to forgive one another, and to serve each other.

Then third, to be mature in Christ is to have clarity about vocation—to know what one is called to speak and do so that at any given time we are able to say, as Christ said in his prayer to the Father, that "I have completed the work that you gave me to do." We learn to live not with frenetic busyness or in despair, but with

---

[2]For a more complete overview of this vision, see Gordon T. Smith, *Called to Be Saints: An Invitation to Christian Maturity* (Downers Grove, IL: InterVarsity Press, 2014).

hope and courage. We live and work in a way that reflects the deep call of God on our lives.

And then, fourth, we need to speak about *emotional* holiness—the capacity to live not with fear or anger or discouragement but with hope that is evident in a resilient joy. When the Spirit is present in our lives, we grow in hope and joy, even in the midst of suffering and difficulty.

This is but one vision of the Christian life and what it means to be mature in Christ. The main point is that if we are speaking about the Spirit, we need to be aware of what we believe the Spirit is up to in our lives, in our world, and in the church. Our pneumatology needs to be about tending to what we recognize the Spirit is doing. Further, the Spirit's work in our lives is not foreign or burdensome. Rather, we long for wisdom; we long to love as we are loved; we long to do good work—the very work we are called to do—and we long to live with a resilient joy. And so, we pray that the Spirit would come and do precisely what the Spirit does: to transform us into the image of Christ.

Maturity in Christ is Not a Self-Help Project

The Scriptures assume something quite extraordinary: that what God created is deeply distorted by sin, and that sin powerfully infects the whole. The world is fragmented, and our only hope is the healing strength of the gospel through the grace of God. But this healing is actually possible; transformation can happen. The human person can be made new—restored to and transformed into the new creation. This transformation will not be complete until the full revelation of Christ, but real change and growth is possible in this life.

More to the point, this transformation is substantive and real. We need to push back against theology that teaches that we are not changed, but that the righteousness of God is imputed to us so that God sees not us but Christ. There is an element of truth in this, of course; our only hope is that God would see us in our new identity in Christ. But we must also insist that the gospel calls us to live a new and transformed life in Christ by the power of the Spirit. We can be and are made new. In Christ, we meet God face-to-face with all the power and freedom of the encounter between Moses and God (see 2 Corinthians 3:12-18). And we are not diminished by this encounter; rather, it radically changes us into new people. We can indeed speak of our transformation, in community, as a child of God. We can and must grow up in our faith.

Thus, there are two different but equally problematic errors we must avoid. One is to *understate* the possibilities of grace and transformation. We need to celebrate the real change that the grace of God can effect in the life of the Christian and the church, and the real change that can come to our world. On the other hand, nothing is gained by *overstating* the possibilities of grace. We know that ultimate transformation will only come when we meet Christ face-to-face. And in the meantime, we will all continue to struggle with our human condition and in humility continue to accept that we are all still on the journey. This awareness does not lead us to despair but to greater dependence on the Spirit.

This is a good thing, in that there are few things so fundamental to a Christian understanding of the ministry of the Spirit as that, however we define the goal of the Christian life, the fulfillment of the human vocation is not the fruit of a self-help project. It is not the Christian equivalent to airport bookstore offerings on how to live a successful life.

Part of the witness of the New Testament is that the Christian life is moving from autonomy and self-dependence to radical dependence on God. The apostle Paul uses the image of the flesh versus Spirit to make this point in two foundational texts in Galatians and Romans. First, the apostle stresses that life "in the flesh" cannot please God; it is the way of death. While we talk of spiritual practices and disciplines and means of grace, they are all precisely so that we can learn to live in intentional dependence on the Spirit.

Then, second, the witness of Romans and Galatians is that we are called to live with a mind set on the Spirit—that is, that by the Spirit we put to death what is within us that is not of God. This is life, and this is the freedom of being children of God. We must live with an intentionality regarding the Spirit, "For all who are led by the Spirit are children of God" (Romans 8:14). Thus, maturity in Christ is the fruit of the Spirit's work in our lives. We learn to lean into and appropriate the grace of God—the grace, in particular, of the Spirit. We know transformation because, over time, we have learned what it means to walk in the Spirit. Isaiah 40 speaks of what it is to live as those who "mount up with wings like eagles" (Isaiah 40:31). However, it has been observed regarding golden eagles that these birds do not travel so far because they have powerful wings that propel them. Rather, their genius is that they catch the updrafts typical of the foothills along their route; they learn to spread their wings and be carried along their journey. For the Christian, we learn to attend to the ways in which the grace of God is present to us. We lean in, depend, and draw strength and hope from the grace of the Spirit in our circumstances.

Living and walking in the Spirit is a journey where we learn to catch the updrafts—the wind of God that carries us as we attend to the presence and power and prompting and inner witness of the Spirit.

Living and Walking in the Spirit

When we speak of living and walking in the Spirit, we first need to consider the question of pace: not just the *way* the Spirit works, but the *timing* of the Spirit in our lives. Then we need to speak of what is called "the means of grace."

A long, slow, gradual, and incremental process. First, we begin with this affirmation: transformation by and in the Spirit is the fruit of a long, slow process. We must learn to avoid being impressed with quick or dramatic outcomes, thinking that if transformation happens instantaneously, it surely means that God must have been at work. While this might well be the way that God chooses to act, typically the Spirit's deep work happens over time. So frequently, "Holy Spirit" talk is about how God worked in some dramatic way to bring about transformation in a moment. And while this is possible, it is not the norm; it is not the usual way in which the Spirit does transformative work in Christians and in the church.

As a rule, transformation is a slow, incremental process. There are no shortcuts. Just as it takes nine months for a baby to emerge from the womb, it takes a lifetime to form a saint in the image of Christ. There will certainly be benchmark events—inflection points in the journey such as a deep awareness of the love of God while on a prayer retreat, a moment of reconciliation between father and daughter that clearly was not the fruit of human effort, a sermon preached where you knew that "this changes everything for me." These are illuminations, gifts from the Spirit that fundamentally alter your worldview. But the deep work of the Spirit—the life-altering work—is more often slow, gradual, and incremental.

The means of grace and habituated practices. Second, we need to consider the "means of grace." What we long for is the living water that quenches our thirst and sustains and renews our souls. But this means we need to tend to the way in which this is received. Many different Christian traditions will speak of the means of grace, but it perhaps had greatest emphasis in John Wesley's theology. He typically used the language of means of grace to speak of those things—as often as not tangible and routine—by which we appropriate the Spirit's grace into our lives. Wesley puts it this way:

> By "means of grace," I understand outward signs, words, or actions, ordained of God, and appointed for this end, to be the ordinary channels whereby He might convey to men, preventing, justifying, or sanctifying grace.
>
> I use this expression, "means of grace," because I know none better; and because it has been generally used in the Christian Church for many ages—in particular by our own Church, which directs us to bless God both for the means of grace, and hope of glory; and teaches us, that a sacrament is "an outward sign of inward grace, and a means whereby we receive the same."
>
> The chief of these means are prayer, whether in secret or with the great congregation; searching the Scriptures (which implies reading, hearing, and meditating thereon); and receiving the Lord's supper, eating bread and drinking wine in remembrance of Him; and these we believe to be ordained of God, as the ordinary channels of conveying His grace to the souls of men.[3]

The means of grace are like the cup that brings the water to our lips; we do not confuse the cup with the water, but we do not despise or discount the cup because it is not the water. It is a means

---

[3]John Wesley, "Sermon XII: The Means of Grace," http://people.exeter.ac.uk/pellison/wesley/vl/12.htm.

to an end: that we would know the living water. This way of thinking is, of course, not unique to Wesley, as he himself stresses in speaking of this perspective as an ancient way of appreciating the ways in which we appropriate the grace of God.

So what are the means of grace, the practices that are the way by which the life of the Spirit is inculcated in our hearts, minds, and bodies? First, there are the *ordained* means of grace—those actions that are mandated by Christ, notably the ministry of the word and the ministry of the table. Following Wesley, preaching and the sacrament of Holy Communion, or the Eucharist, are foundational. Note the biblical precedent here: following the day of Pentecost, the early church devoted themselves to the apostles' teaching and the breaking of the bread, that is, the Lord's Table (Acts 2:42). They could not live the Pentecost-informed and infused life if they neglected these fundamental and ordained practices. Or, stating it positively, they lived in the grace and dynamic presence of the Spirit in their midst by being a people of word and table. A church that seeks to live in the grace and power of the Spirit will be demarcated by these routine actions. In the coming chapters on the Holy Spirit and the church, these will be a particular focus.

But then we can also speak of other practices that are the means by which the Spirit is present in our lives: weekly sabbath observance, daily early morning prayer with the Psalms, the long walk or even a pilgrimage, a conversation with a spiritual director or a spiritual friend. Each of us should ask, Where am I attending to those means of grace that are essential or imperative in my life circumstance? As Father Thomas Ryan put it in conversation with me: "What are the pillars that hold up the roof of your spiritual house?"

Yes, the grace of God is always sufficient for whatever circumstance we might have to journey through. But we cannot presume on the grace of God; we must attend to the means by which that grace is given to us. We must be sure that the pillars are in place in our lives such that we are growing and maturing in the faith. They are *not* means by which we self-construct our lives, but, they are no less essential. We will not grow and mature in the faith—we will not be led by the Spirit and walk in the Spirit—without them.

The means of grace within a Christian community are an integral part of the daily and weekly routines of our lives; they are routine and repeated practices. Our understanding of the work and ministry of the Holy Spirit—pneumatology—has been deeply strengthened by the movement of the last two or three decades that has given particular focus to spiritual practice and the cultivation of virtue. Building on the work of Alasdair MacIntyre, a vibrant conversation has been sustained by several key voices that merit our attention, including Miroslav Volf, Dorothy Bass, Greg Jones, Craig Dykstra, and others.[4] These writers have stressed that faith and virtue are formed through routinized actions that are a vehicle through which faith and the life of faith is formed—what Dykstra and Bass call "patterned activities,"[5] or what others speak of as *habituated practices.*

The point is that the work of the Spirit is cultivated within our hearts, minds, and bodies through intentional spiritual discipline. There is a place for the immediate and the spontaneous in our worship, our relationships, and in our work, of course. But we do

---

[4]Consider two publications in particular: *Practicing Our Faith: A Way of Life for a Searching People,* ed. Dorothy C. Bass and Craig Dykstra (San Francisco: Jossey-Bass, 1997); and *Practicing Theology: Beliefs and Practices in Christian Life,* ed. Miroslav Volf and Dorothy C. Bass (Grand Rapids, MI: Eerdmans, 2002).

[5]Dykstra and Bass, *Practicing Theology,* 26.

not assume that this somehow transcends or is more spiritual than the ordinary, the mundane, and the routine. Women and men who walk in the Spirit recognize the value not so much of living spontaneously as of living a life that is marked by consistent practices over an extended season. They are part of a community of faith that attends to word and table as well as the regular communal practices of eager hospitality and generous service. They have their routines that mark their lives and by which virtue is formed within them—through the gracious ministry of the Spirit.

The *positive* emphasis on those actions by which we lean into the Spirit's ministry needs to be complemented by those spiritual practices that go against the grain of the culture or our own proclivities— elements of our social setting or our personal inclinations that are antithetical to our faith. We need to recognize that a regular visit to a mall may well cultivate a consumeristic mindset that we perhaps need to starve—that is, to deny that within us that is not of the Spirit. These are typically spoken of as *ascetical* practices—those routinized actions by which we choose to not be conformed to this world so that we can be transformed by the renewal of our minds (Romans 12:1-2). We ask ourselves if there are habits or routinized actions that, while part of our culture, we recognize to be what we might call *mal*-practices. But this is all with the reminder that the deep work of the Spirit is slow, gradual, and incremental.

Praying in the Spirit

There is a broad consensus in the history of the church that nothing is so foundational, no practice of the Christian life is more pivotal, than the discipline of regular prayer. Our prayers are an essential means by which we walk in the Spirit. In Ephesians 6:18 we read the apostolic exhortation to "pray in the Spirit at all times in every prayer and supplication." Prayer in the Spirit is not some special, unique, or charismatic kind of prayer. It is, in fact, the only way to pray. But this does suggest that in our praying we are not only speaking to God but also responding to the witness and prompting of the Spirit. Further, prayer is a learned art or practice. We can and must learn to pray and attend to our prayers if we are going to mature in and through the grace of the Spirit.

How can we cultivate the capacity and disposition, in worship and in work, of attending to the inner promptings of the Spirit and recognizing the way in which the Spirit is present in our world? How can we see the Spirit before us as we go, beside us as we navigate our circumstances and challenges, and within us granting us clarity of conviction and courage to do what we are called to do and say what needs to be said? Can we be attentive through times of difficulty and suffering, when it is most challenging to lift up our hearts to God—that is, when pain or disappointment seemingly overcome us?

Doing this is a habit of the heart. We learn to attend by attending; we learn to pray in the Spirit by deciding that this is the manner in which we will engage our own lives and our world. We choose to walk and live and respond and pray as those who recognize the immediacy of the Spirit in our hearts and in our circumstances. We see and feel the intersection of heaven and earth as something that is not so much extraordinary but as actually routine. Thus in Romans 8:26-27 we read: "In the same way, the Spirit helps us in our weakness. We do not know what we ought to pray for, but the Spirit himself intercedes for us through wordless groans. And he who searches our hearts knows the mind of the Spirit, because the Spirit intercedes for God's people in accordance with the will of God" (NIV).

This is fundamental to our understanding of prayer and our experience of the Spirit. In our prayer we are not alone; the Spirit groans *with* us. Also, this reference to groaning is a reminder that the Spirit is not merely concerned for our personal well-being but is eagerly longing for the renewal of all creation. Then, further, we surely cannot read Romans 8:26 except in light of Romans 8:17, which speaks of how we are joint heirs with Christ. Our suffering and difficulties—an inevitable part of our Christian experience— are windows by which we are drawn into the company of Christ through the grace of the Spirit, who groans with us in our time of difficulty and darkness. The reference to "wordless groans" alerts us to the simple reality that prayer is not to be reduced to words offered to God; rather, in the Spirit our prayers are often but our deep yearning, our deep longing for the fulfillment of God's purposes in our world, in our lives, and in the lives of those we love and care for.

Thus, in the Spirit we can pray—giving thanks, making confession, and intentionally discerning the call and purposes of the Spirit in our lives and in our work.[6] Each dimension of our praying is very much one of responding, intentionally, to the Spirit: the Spirit gives us eyes to see the goodness of God for which we might give thanks; the Spirit is the gift by which we know ourselves and come to confession; and the Spirit guides us in times of choice. We move from hectic business on the one hand and despair on the other and graciously accept where God is calling us to speak and act. With open hearts and minds, we attend to the quiet witness of the Spirit and learn discernment. We know that

---

[6]For a fuller treatment of this approach to prayer in the Spirit—thanksgiving, confession, and discernment—see Gordon T. Smith, *Teach Us to Pray* (Downers Grove, IL: InterVarsity Press, 2018).

not every impression, every movement of the heart, is from God. Thus we must test everything; we intentionally cultivate a healthy self-suspicion; we learn to be alert to the snake who masquerades as an angel of light (2 Corinthians 11:14). Discernment requires that we be accountable to others, that we know what it means to examine our motives, and, further, that we lean into the witness of the Scriptures. Along the way, we hesitate to make a one-to-one assumption that the Lord led us to do this or that or the other. Humility demands that we do not presume and casually speak of how the Lord has guided us; we just do what we sense the Spirit is prompting us to do, knowing that we will not always get it right. But, over time and with practice, we will come to an increasing capacity to know and respond to the inner witness of the Spirit.

THROUGH SICKNESS AND HEALTH;
THROUGH HEALING AND LOSS

Our Christian spiritual heritage has always had within it a stream that has recognized that the grace of the Holy Spirit is not limited to interior matters of the heart but also impacts our physical health and well-being. Many, for example, especially within the Holiness-Pentecostal tradition, have affirmed that the Spirit of God is eager and willing to bring healing and restoration in the face of sickness. We only need to ask and trust the Spirit to bring healing.

James 5 speaks of the ministry of elders for the laying on of hands and the prayer of faith that those who are sick might know healing and wholeness. This is an integral way in which the Spirit graces the body. It is in direct continuity with the healing ministry of Jesus—in the power of the Spirit—and the healing ministry of the apostles, as referenced in the book of Acts, coming directly out the way in which the church was and continues to be empowered by the Spirit. Also in 1 Corinthians, "gifts of healing" is mentioned three times as one of the ways in which the Holy Spirit is gracing the church (1 Corinthians 12:9, 28, 30).

Three observations and comments follow from this. First, prayers for healing are not only appropriate and fitting but perhaps actually expected and commanded. It would appear from James 5 that this is to actually be part of the practice of the church: the laying on of hands; the confident prayer of faith; the expectation of grace for the body.

Second, it is a problem and a distraction when the practice of anointing the sick becomes either a public spectacle or is viewed as a sign that God is showing grace or special favor to a church or an individual. We can affirm the legitimate place of the anointing of the sick, but this practice must be integral to congregational life and accompanied by the interior work of confession and inner renewal, as we see in James 5. Thus, why not make it a regular part of the liturgy? Christ Church Cathedral in Vancouver, for example, gives opportunity for anointing in a side chapel every Sunday during the celebration of the Eucharist. When I served as the pastor of Union Church of Manila, we let it be known that after the service elders were available to any who wished to be anointed and prayed for.

Third, it is imperative that any teaching on the grace of healing be matched by a similar call to know the grace of God in suffering and sickness. The persecuted church has no illusions on this score; God often allows his church and his people to walk through dark valleys. Some might indeed know a special touch of healing in their bodies; many—perhaps most—will instead experience the loss of a child, the debilitating effects of cancer, or some other ailment for which the call of the hour is patience, perseverance, and a deepening faith in God even in the midst of pain—indeed, particularly in the midst of the pain.

We only have a genuinely biblical pneumatology if we have a theology of suffering; any articulation of a vision for strength and healing for the body needs to be found side by side with a similar articulation of what it means to be joint heirs with Christ in his suffering (Romans 8:17). The two must go together. A deep confidence in the ministry of the Spirit must include an appreciation for how the Spirit is present to us in both sickness and health—indeed, in the remarkable words of Romans 8:26-27, the Spirit groans with us with sighs too deep for words. We cannot yield to any temptation to overstate what the Spirit will do—not so much what the Spirit *can* do, which is all things, but what the Spirit *chooses* to do—this side of the fulfillment of the reign of God.

Our greatest need is not the healing of the body but rather that we would be united with Christ in his death and resurrection. The text that speaks to how the Spirit witnesses with our spirits that we are children of God leads directly into the affirmation that in our suffering we are joint heirs of Christ in his suffering (Rom 8:17). Through times of difficulty and suffering, united with Christ, we can indeed know the deep consolation of the Spirit of God—the peace that transcends all understanding. And more, it is particularly in times of difficulty and trial that we must be particularly faithful in the practices by which we know the grace of the Spirit in our lives.

CONCLUSION

In any and all conversations about the Holy Spirit, we need to ask: What is the evidence that we are in tune with the Spirit and what the Spirit is doing in our lives? It all comes back to our understanding of what we mean by maturity in Christ. What is the content of this maturity? What is our shared vocation, and to what end have we been created?

I have suggested that the evidence of the Spirit's grace in our lives will be:

- We are growing in wisdom, including moral intelligence.

- We are learning to love others as Christ has loved us.

- We have vocational clarity, knowing what we are to say and not say, what we are to do and what does not need to be done.

- We are growing in our capacity to live and work with a resilient joy and a vibrant hope, even in the midst of difficulty and suffering.

Most of all, in the Spirit we increasingly come to union with Christ. In and by the Spirit, we come to know Christ more fully, love Christ more deeply, and, to serve Christ with greater generosity. Christ is formed within us.

This means that we come to a humble and greater self-awareness—living not in illusion or pretense or narcissism, but with a radical other-centeredness—living for Christ and for others. It is this longing for freedom in Christ that leads us to pray, "Welcome, Holy Spirit."

CHAPTER SIX

THE SPIRIT AND THE WORD

O NE'S UNDERSTANDING OF THE SPIRIT and experience of the grace of the Spirit is in many respects dependent on four key questions. Two have been addressed so far—
how the Spirit relates to Christ and how the Spirit relates to
creation. In the following two chapters, we will consider the relationship of the Spirit with the church. But before we move into
those chapters, we need to have some clarity on the relationship
between the Spirit and the Word.

Colossians and Ephesians are similar but different in notable
ways, and the contrast and comparison between the two can be
instructive. In addressing some of the same themes, these two
books of the Bible seem to consider them from a slightly different
angle. One intriguing example of this is where the apostle Paul
calls for common worship in song, with gratitude. In Ephesians,
this segment begins with "be filled with the Spirit": "Be filled with
the Spirit, as you sing psalms and hymns and spiritual songs
among yourselves, singing and making melody to the Lord in your
hearts, giving thanks to God the Father at all times for everything
in the name of our Lord Jesus Christ" (Ephesians 5:18-20).

The Colossians counterpart opens not with "be filled with the
Spirit" but with a reference to the Word: "Let the word of Christ
dwell in you richly; teach and admonish one another in all

wisdom; and with gratitude in your hearts sing psalms, hymns, and spiritual songs to God. And whatever you do, in word or deed, do everything in the name of the Lord Jesus, giving thanks to God the Father through him" (Colossians 3:16-17).

Which is it? By what means or grace is it that our worship is truly to the Father, through the Son, with gratitude infusing our songs of praise? Is it "be filled with the Spirit," or "Let the word of Christ dwell in you richly"? This is a false choice; it is necessarily both/and. This illustrates powerfully the ways in which we need to speak about the Word and the Spirit—the Word as God speaking, including through the Scriptures, and the Spirit as the breath of God, the third person of the Trinity, informing, animating, and illuminating the Word and bringing that Word into our minds and hearts so that it truly is a life-giving and transformative Word.

Our theology of the Spirit and our theology of the Word—our understanding of the third person of the Trinity, on the one hand, and our understanding of the Scriptures in the life of the church, on the other, including the character and the authority of Scripture—are *interdependent*. We do not have a theology of Scripture without a dynamic pneumatology; we do not have a biblical theology of the Spirit without its counterpart, the theology of Scripture. The two are understood in light of the other.

This counterpoint between Word and Spirit is actually built into the fabric of creation. As noted in chapter 3, at creation Word and Spirit operate in dynamic interplay to bring about the creative and redemptive purposes of God—the wind of God swept over the waters of the earth as God said, "Let there be . . ." (Genesis 1:2-3). The Psalms then echo this and speak of Word and breath as the means by which the heavens came into being—reflecting the speaking of God and the hovering of the Spirit when all things were brought into being. Thus the psalmist declares:

By the word of the LORD the heavens were made,
and all their host by the breath of his mouth. (Psalm 33:6)

Then further, the incarnation is an action of Word and Spirit— with the Spirit coming over Mary as the Word became flesh and dwelt among us (John 1:14).

Here, though, we are giving attention to the relationship between the Spirit and the Scriptures. And to this end, we will consider three things. First, the Scriptures are Spirit-inspired; it is thus that the Bible is a sacred text with unique authority in the life of the church and the life of the Christian. Second, Word and Spirit function in tandem; here we give special consideration to how the Word is an essential vehicle by which the Spirit is present to the church and to the Christian. Third, we read the Scriptures in a manner that is informed and illuminated by the Spirit.

THE SCRIPTURES AS INSPIRED BY THE SPIRIT

When we consider the relationship between the Word and the Spirit, we begin by noting that the Scriptures themselves testify to their own unique character. We have the affirmation that the prophets and the apostles spoke and wrote under inspiration of the Spirit. Thus we read: "All Scripture is inspired by God and is useful for teaching, for reproof, for correction, and for training in righteousness, so that everyone who belongs to God may be proficient, equipped for every good work" (2 Timothy 3:16-17).

Scripture is animated and infused by—we might say *inspirited* by—the Holy Spirit. As such, it has unique authority within the life and witness of the community of faith; it is trustworthy; it is the sacred text that establishes, informs, reforms, and transforms the life, worship, and witness of the church. Thus we rightly speak of this text as "the Word of the Lord." It is the Word of God; it is the Word of Christ.

This does not take away from its human character. The Bible is still a deeply human book. In the same way that Christ himself is fully divine and fully human, and his humanity in no way compromises or diminishes his deity, the Scriptures have both a divine and human character to them. The Bible is not God, but the Christian spiritual and intellectual tradition has always affirmed the unique character of this book in that it is inspired by the Spirit—the apostles and prophets spoke under the guidance and animating grace of the Spirit. Thus we speak of the Bible as the Word of God. And yet, at the same time the prophets and apostles were of their time and place; they were located in spiritual historical circumstances, lived within specific cultures, and each one was a distinctive personality. The apostle Paul's unique circumstances and personality consistently come through in his letters—particularly when he is so personal in 2 Corinthians. The point is that the human character of the Scriptures does not diminish or undermine our capacity to know God through the ancient Word. Rather, just as to know Jesus as the Son of God is to encounter Jesus in all his humanity, in like manner the human character of the Scriptures is the means by which we know the Bible as the Word of God.

Thus we read and preach the Scriptures with no apology for their deep humanity. We attend to the ways in which the Scriptures arose and see that they only make sense against the background of the time and place in which they were composed. This is why we must affirm that an intellectual reading of Scripture, a thoughtful reading where we engage and foster a Christian mind, is pivotal for the formation of the Christian life. Pastors who preach in the inspiration of the Holy Spirit are preachers who have learned what the pastoral epistles speak of as handling the word of truth rightly (2 Timothy 2:15). Spirit-anointed preaching is evident in thoughtful engagement with the biblical text, in careful exegesis, and in a deep respect for the text as it has come to us.

THE SPIRIT AND SCRIPTURE IN TANDEM

Part of the genius of God's redemptive work in the world—in creation but also in the renewal and transformation of all things— is how the Spirit and the Scriptures function in tandem. We see this in particular in the way that the apostle Paul speaks of the ministry of preaching—his own and that of the early church. Thus in 1 Thessalonians 1:5 he speaks of his confidence that the fruit of his ministry was the interplay of Word and Spirit: "Our message of the gospel came to you not in word only, but also in power and in the Holy the Spirit." They received the word with confidence and joy and the willingness to suffer persecution. And in 1 Corinthians 2:4, Paul observes that his preaching was as "a demonstration of Spirit and of power." This was not because it was particularly loud or bold or charismatic, but because, as he put it elsewhere, he simply sought to let the truth of the Scriptures be compelling in its own right (2 Corinthians 4:2), and, of course, because he resolved to preach Christ and him crucified. Ephesians 6:17 speaks of how the sword of the Spirit is the Word of God. In the Gospels, Jesus affirms that "the words that I have spoken to you are spirit and life" (John 6:63). The church is sanctified by the Spirit; the church is sanctified by the Word—by the truth (John 17:17).

It is by the Spirit that the Word illumines, rekindles, and strengthens. It is by the Spirit that the Scriptures are not merely print on paper, but a life-giving Word. Without the Spirit, the Bible is just ink on a page. Therefore, all engagement with the text must be intentional, leaning into and dependent on the Spirit who guides, teaches, illumines, and convicts. The Spirit remains fully present not only to the process of inspiration and canonization but also in the reading, interpretation, proclamation, and living out of the sacred text.

It is thus by the Spirit that the Word becomes nourishment and grace for the people of God. Both "be filled with the Spirit" and "let the word of Christ dwell in you richly" speak to *interiority*. Each calls us to a living from the depths—from the heart. Being *filled* and being *indwelt* function together, and interiority is the fruit of their joint operation. The Word becomes interior through the grace of the Spirit, and the only Spirit we know is the Spirit whose transformative work in our lives is *through* the sacred text.

And so, for example, Romans 5:8 speaks of how the love of God is demonstrated in this—that Christ died for us while we were yet sinners. But this comes with the affirmation that the love of God is poured into our hearts by the Holy Spirit (Romans 5:5). It is by the Spirit that we not only see and appreciate, but then also know and *feel* to the depths of our beings that we are loved. The revelation of the cross of Christ—the truth of the cross—is made interior and thus made *transformative* in our lives through the ministry of the Spirit. The Scriptures assure us that we are children of God, but it is the Spirit, in the powerful language of Romans 8:16, that "witness[es] with our spirit that we are children of God." It is always both/and.

Thus we refuse to pit word, text, intellect, exegesis, and careful, thoughtful reading of Scripture over against the movements of the heart. The genius of Christian spirituality is found in the interplay of head and heart, intellect and affect. Part of how we demonstrate this is by a consideration of the relationship between the Spirit and the Word.

This relationship between Word and Spirit was a particular emphasis of the Protestant reformers, especially John Calvin. What this meant for him was that the revelation of God was *dynamic* rather than static. It is not that the Spirit inspired the text and said, "You're good to go, and we'll meet again when Christ returns." Rather, there is an *immediacy* between Word and Spirit in the experience of the Christian and of the church.

Calvin comes at the relationship between the Spirit and the Word assuming that faith is the heart of the matter—both in coming to a knowledge of God in Christ and in the emerging life of Christ. As he puts it, "Faith is the principal work of the Holy Spirit."[1] It is all of faith, and faith is nurtured through hearing— through the ear that hears the Word of God.[2]

But this is no mere human exercise; rather, the illumination of the mind and the confirmation of the heart happens through another agent, one might say. What is revealed to the mind and sealed in the heart is by the Holy Spirit.[3] And for Calvin, they go together—head and heart, knowledge and what he speaks of as "pious disposition."[4]

Thus we need to avoid what we might speak of as biblicism: the proclivity to be committed to biblical authority and the significance of the text but without the dynamic of the Spirit's presence

[1] John Calvin, *Institutes of the Christian Religion*, ed. John T. McNeill, trans. Ford Lewis Battles (Louisville, KY: Westminster John Knox Press, 2011), 3.1.4 (541).
[2] Calvin, *Institutes*, 3.2.6 (548-49).
[3] Calvin, *Institutes*, 3.2.7 (550).
[4] Calvin, *Institutes*, 3.2.8 (553).

in our reading, our preaching, and our living of the text. We do not defend the authority of the Bible except in also speaking of the Spirit by whom the text is made present to the hearts and minds of the people of God. There are two equal and troublesome tendencies that are both current, it seems, in each generation of the life of the church: to read the Bible as text without the immediacy of the Spirit, or to seek to be attentive to the Spirit with only a selective or imposed reading of the text—not letting the text itself be a means by which the Spirit works in our lives, in the church, and in the world.

The first is the tendency of the biblicist who treats the Bible as a kind of static holy book. As John Calvin stressed, "Without the illumination of the Holy Spirit, the Word can do nothing."[5] The point in this is that it is in the immediate; this is not about the original inspiration of the Scriptures. Rather, in our reading and preaching the illuminating ministry of the Spirit brings about both understanding in the intellect *and* confirmation in the heart.[6] Thus we eschew biblicist rationalism, which approaches the Scriptures without taking into account the immediacy of the Spirit in our reading and interpretation. In his little book *The Divine Conquest*, A. W. Tozer speaks to the ways in which the Spirit is present to us—in real time, illuminating and guiding the church and the Christian community into truth. At a time when fundamentalism was equated with the conservative side of the "conservative-liberal" debates of the 1950s, Tozer is scathing in his critique of fundamentalism due to what he calls the "error of textualism"—and the danger of being "Bible taught" and not Spirit taught.[7]

---

[5]Calvin, *Institutes*, 3.2.33 (580).
[6]Calvin, *Institutes*, 3.2.36 (583-84).
[7]A. W. Tozer, *The Divine Conquest* (Harrisburg, PA: Christian Publications, 1950), 78-79.

Of course, he was not suggesting that we only attend to the Spirit. Rather, his point is that we cannot read the Scriptures and hear them except in the immediacy of our relationship with the Holy Spirit, or, as he puts it, "There is no truth apart from the Spirit."[8] By this Tozer does not mean that the Scriptures are authoritative because they are Spirit-inspired—which he would certainly affirm. Rather, he is speaking of the *immediacy* of the Spirit in our learning, our encounter with the Word, and thus with the truth.

When we lose the attentiveness to the Spirit in our reading and preaching, we seem to lose our capacity for humility in both. We assume that our reading is the final and authoritative reading, and the result is often a loss of continuous learning and, further, a propensity to use the Bible as a tool to harp away at those who differ with us.

But the solution to this is not that we are so "Spirit-directed" that we assume the immediacy of the Spirit allows us to either completely ignore the Scriptures or use them in a way that they are only about finding inspiration. On the one hand, we have the biblicist. On the other, we have those who read selectively; they read and preach without regard for the careful exegesis of the text but only for what seemingly moves them. They need the reminder that true charismatic, Spirit in-filled worship is not merely about ecstatic song, but also about the careful exposition of Scripture. Just as we avoid the biblicist error, we must resist the sentimentalism or subjectivism that is all about experience and that only uses the Scriptures in a manner that does not genuinely engage the text. The genius of the Christian tradition is the engagement

---

[8]Tozer, *Divine Conquest*, 79.

of head and heart, Word and Spirit, intellect and affect, scholarship and prayer, exegesis and illumination through the inner witness. We can fully affirm the experiential while always having an unequivocal affirmation of the priority of Scripture in the life of the church.

To summarize, a church that is deeply committed to the transforming work of the Spirit will be devoted to the apostles' teaching (Acts 2:42). They walk in the Spirit, and this is evident, in part, in their commitment to the oral reading of Scripture and to preaching the word in season and out of season (2 Timothy 4:2). The faithful and consistent reading and exposition will mark their shared life; it will be central to their worship and it will be evident in their commitment to the study of the Scriptures and to the ways in which they equip new Christians to learn to read the Bible for themselves. Indeed, they cannot walk in the Spirit if they are not women and men of the Word.

Scholarly preaching is essential—by which I mean preaching that is thoughtfully engaged with the text. Without any apology, we can insist that when we preach in full dependence on the illuminating work of the Spirit, precisely because we are doing this in dependence on the Spirit, we engage minds. We are thoughtful. We reject any idea that we would bifurcate scholarship from Spirit-anointed preaching. The two necessarily go together: the grace we seek is careful, thoughtful engagement with the text under the gracious ministry of the Holy Spirit. Our radical dependence on the Spirit will not in any way lead us to disparage the text, which, of course, is Spirit-inspired. We must be alert to those who think that deep transformation comes by telling inspiring stories—as though what transforms is an account of someone who has had a tremendous experience and that in like manner we might be open to such an experience. Those who "preach" in this way seem to think that telling an inspiring story about what God has done will, in itself, bring about deep change.

The problem with this approach is that most of the deep work of God happens through the slow, gradual, and incremental, not through the dramatic and exciting. The danger is that we then try to keep upping the ante with exciting stories while missing the ways the Spirit is present and active through the valleys and through the times of difficulty and suffering.

Thus, the Scriptures are read and proclaimed; the ancient text is made present to the people of God, week in and week out. This is not about entertainment; it is, rather, a thoughtful engagement with the transforming power of the Word. We let Word and Spirit do what only the Word and Spirit can do. We trust the Word; we trust the Spirit. We are patient; we are confident that, as put so exquisitely by the prophet Isaiah, in the Spirit the Word "shall not return . . . empty" but shall accomplish the purpose for which it has been sent (Isaiah 55:11). We turn from thinking that it is charismatic preaching with inspiring stories that brings about transformation; rather, what transforms is not the personality of the preacher but the power of the Word made alive and present to the hearer by the grace of the Spirit.

THE IMMEDIACY OF THE SPIRIT IN READING AND LIVING THE SCRIPTURES

In John 16, Jesus tells his disciples that he has much more to say to them, but it is more than they can bear, and that the Spirit of truth "will guide you into all the truth" (John 16:13). The canon of Scripture is closed; the Scriptures as given have a regulatory role in the life and witness of the church and the experience of each individual Christian. Apostolic revelation—as housed in Scripture—remains the baseline, and we can live confident that, in the language of 2 Timothy 3:16, this ancient text is indeed sufficient for our lives and for the knowledge of God's salvation. With this basic conviction, we can then also affirm two things. First, the words of Jesus suggest that in our reading and preaching and living of the text, we foster a radical dependence on the Spirit. We ask: How must this text be read and preached, in this time and in this place? How is the Spirit now, today, for this context and setting, calling us to engage the truth? When we engage the Scriptures with this disposition of heart and mind, we find that our engagement with the text is an iterative one: each reading takes us deeper; our understanding each time through becomes more nuanced. We come back to familiar texts and now, by the illuminating grace of the Spirit, we see and hear them in a different light. We find that we are surprised, yet again, by the ancient truth.

Then, second, we also learn to read the text not in isolation but in community. We listen to how others read the same familiar texts and perhaps see and read them differently. We read the text with those who are at the margins or with those of other cultures, or as older Christians we listen to how younger Christians are reading the text. We see this engagement, this listening to the other, as a way by which the Spirit is opening up our eyes and our hearts to a reading of the text that we had not appreciated and perhaps could not have seen earlier. This does not mean we have an open canon or new revelation; rather, we are recognizing that the ancient text is ever new to us. We see further the more we have lived in the text in intentional dependence on the guidance and illuminating work of the Spirit, and read the text in community and with genuine accountability to others.

I must stress that the Word is the servant of the Spirit; it is the means by which the Spirit works and ministers in the church and in the world. But then we also see that the Spirit is the servant of the Word, illuminating and opening up heart and mind to see, appreciate, and live the Word.

Each generation of Christians must read the text, in the Spirit, for itself. The truths of Scripture are not passed down as a static object like a baton from one generation to the next. Rather, while each generation reads the text, in the Spirit, in deep continuity with the past, with their Christian heritage, it is still a *new* reading. Now we read the Scriptures, attentive to the past but present to the here and now, attending to and dependent on the Spirit to illumine hearts and minds for this time and this place.

There is likely no more dramatic an example of this than the Council of Jerusalem described for us in Acts 15. The issue at hand is whether Gentiles need to become Jews before they can become Christians, and whether Jewish practices are required of all Christians. Paul had returned from his missionary endeavors in Asia Minor and was making the case that Gentiles could be Christian without first becoming Jewish. It is important to note that those who argued against this move did so by appealing to Scripture. Indeed, they referenced the authority of the prophet Moses (Acts 15:1). The counterproposal from Paul and Barnabas required a fresh reading of the Hebrew Scriptures. For most of those present, it would have been assumed that Jewish practices —liturgical and otherwise—are the baseline for what it means to be Christian. But by the grace of the Spirit, they came to a new reading, a new vision of what God was doing in the world. It was by the Spirit that they could come to the conclusion that "it seemed good to the Holy Spirit and to us" (Acts 15:28) that they would not impose an undue burden on the new Gentile Christian community.

Might this then mean that each culture needs to read the text, from its social and economic context, in the Spirit? Native Americans, Maori New Zealanders, and indigenous Canadians will not likely be reading the text the way that their settler neighbors read the text. They will read it for themselves. A missionary may well take the message of the gospel to a people who hear it for the first time, and in so doing introduce new believers to the Scriptures. But in time, as those in the church mature, they will be empowered to read the Bible for themselves, or, more accurately, to read the text with the guidance of the Spirit. The missionary then becomes a learner, as now one who first brought the gospel to these people hears the Scriptures read and interpreted through their eyes and ears and experience.

That is, we learn from one another. Euro-Canadians listen to how both indigenous Canadians and new immigrants to Canada are reading the text. Korean missionaries to Southeast Asia attend to how those whom they are serving are now reading the text in the guidance of the Spirit and seeing perspectives and vistas beyond what they—as foreign missionaries—were seeing in the text. We are all learners, and so we hold our deep convictions regarding the meaning of texts firmly but lightly—always open to the ways in which the Spirit is continuing to teach the church. Thus I ask those who are older: Can we come alongside an emerging generation of leaders in Africa, Latin America, Asia, and the Middle East, and not only be their mentors but also be learners with them and from them, as they, immersed in the Scriptures, attend to the witness of the Spirit? Can I, as a Euro-Canadian, read the text with fresh eyes that are given to me by those from the Global South through the gracious work of the Spirit in my heart and mind?[9]

All of this suggests that we need to be intentional in our receptivity to the Spirit—open to the witness of the Spirit in the here and now. We ask, not alone but in community, "What is the Spirit saying to the church?" And then, of course, "What is the Spirit saying to me, personally, through the Scriptures?" We ask what the Spirit of God is witnessing to now, in this time and this place, in our lives and in our community and in our world.

That may seem a bit unsettling. We would like the truth to be given, once and for all—fixed, static, unambiguous. However, the Bible is a living text when we read it as it was meant to be read: in the Spirit. This means that we read in the presence and power of the One who is pushing boundaries and borders and giving us new vistas, new perspectives, new challenges—but always with and for those who are attentive to and deeply indwelt by the Word (Colossians 3:16).

CONCLUSION

This calls for intentionality. In our personal prayers we open the sacred text with the prayer, "Come, Holy Spirit, come." We pray that the Spirit will be present to us in our reading and give us courage and grace and a radical openness to the inner witness of

---

[9]Here are some examples of alternate readings of Scripture—of hearing the Scriptures through the eyes, ears, and experience of others. From the Australian Aboriginal experience, Graham Paulson and Mark Bett, "Five Smooth Stones: Reading the Bible Through Aboriginal Eyes," where they speak of "two-way learning," https://repository.divinity.edu.au/1672/1/Brett_M_Five_Smooth_Stones_BUV_edit.pdf. See also Esau McCaulley, *Reading While Black: African American Biblical Interpretation as an Exercise in Hope* (Downers Grove, IL: IVP Academic, 2020). And to hear from both sides of the Israel-Palestine experience of the land, consider *Through My Enemy's Eyes: Envisioning Reconciliation in Israel-Palestine*, by Salim J. Munayer and Lisa Loden—a Palestinian Christian and an Israeli Messianic Jew (Milton Keynes: Paternoster, 2014).

the Spirit that convicts of sin and brings insight and new learning. The relationship with the Scriptures is dynamic, not static; we are ever learning and ever being challenged in our own personal reading and in our reading with others, especially those of other cultural and social backgrounds.

In our weekly worship, we affirm the primacy of the Scriptures in the liturgy—the reading of the Old Testament, the Epistles, and the Gospels, and then the weekly preached Word. What follows from all of this is that we pray and invoke the present and illuminating grace of the Spirit as we come to the proclamation of the Word. We offer the prayer that is surely an essential element in the liturgy: the prayer for illumination. We always come to the text—read and proclaimed—praying for the Holy Spirit to come with some variation of, "Oh Father, by your Word and by your Spirit, illumine our hearts, rekindle our hearts, and strengthen our wills; we ask this in the name of the risen and ascended Lord Jesus Christ."

Do we need to do this prayer for illumination *every* time we come to the Word? Why not? But more to the point, our default inclination is to assume that we can make our understanding and engagement with the text happen. We so easily default to thinking that we can understand what we are reading and make sense of it. Thus, I suggest, we need to come back again and again to our deep dependence on the Spirit. Why not choose to signal this *every* time we come to the text of Scripture in our individual prayers, and every time in our corporate worship that we come to our shared reading and preaching of Scripture? Why not welcome the Holy Spirit, praying, "Come, Holy Spirit, come"?

CHAPTER SEVEN

THE SPIRIT AND
THE CHURCH LOCAL

*I*T IS OFTEN SAID that the day of Pentecost is the birthday of the church. This is true, in a sense, but it is a partial truth. One could just as easily make the case that the church was established with the ascension, when Christ was established as Lord of all and as head of the church. Or perhaps it is both together, in that the church—the new covenant people of God—is distinctly the fruit of the outpouring of the gift of the Spirit. With the ascension and with the gift of the Spirit, the church is established. Thus in the Nicene Creed, when we say, "I believe in the Spirit, the Lord and Giver of Life," this necessarily means—within the same article of faith—that we affirm that we "believe in one, holy, catholic and apostolic church." The two go together. The ascended Lord sent the Spirit so that the church can be the body of Christ and the people of God—so that the church can be one, holy, catholic, and apostolic.

Therefore, we must speak of an *ecclesial* pneumatology—that is, our understanding of the Holy Spirit is informed and shaped by our understanding of the church: that our understanding of and experience of the Spirit that is intentionally churchly—rooted in the life and witness of the community of faith.[1] While the ministry

---

[1]The term "pneumatological ecclesiology" originates with Yves Congar, the great Roman Catholic theologian who had such a profound impact on Vatican II and made significant

of the Spirit is not confined to either the physical boundaries or the speaking and actions of the church, it is not an overstatement to say that we are not in fellowship with the Spirit if we are not in fellowship with the church. Or, stating it positively, to walk in the Spirit is to live intentionally as part of the church. Christian religious experience is by its nature not only subjective, personal, and interior, as many assume, but also corporate and communal. It is interior experience that is moderated and mediated by word and sacrament—by rites and rituals of the common or shared life of the church. Even in our personal journey—for example, our solitary prayers—we are in community.

Again, then, the presence and work of the Spirit leads to materiality: creation, incarnation, and then on the day of Pentecost Christ sends the Spirit and thereby brings into being the church as a flesh and blood people bound together in common faith, sustained by a physical and tangible meal. They are the body of Christ. Thus we need to reflect on what the ministry of the Spirit means concretely in the life, worship, governance, and mission of the church. To this end, it is helpful to turn to the book of Ephesians—in many respects the foundational text for what we mean by an "ecclesial pneumatology."

Ephesians profiles the connection between the ascension and the ministry of the Spirit. We see the relationship between the Spirit and the church through the lens of ascension—that is, our

contributions as an ecumenist, but particularly in the way he addressed the integration of the theology of the church with the theology of the Spirit. Actually, his ecumenism and his pneumatological ecclesiology come together, as he himself noted: "In this task [the study of the Spirit and the church] I have derived great benefit from the encouragement given by my Orthodox friends and from the reading of the church Fathers." Yves M. J. Congar, *The Word and the Spirit*, trans. David Smith (San Francisco: Harper & Row, 1986). See in particular volume 2 of his major three-volume contribution to pneumatology: Yves M. J. Congar, *I Believe in the Holy Spirit*, trans. David Smith (New York: Seabury, 1983; Crossroads, 1997).

ecclesial pneumatology emerges from the central and defining place of Christ in the church and in the cosmos. Ephesians 1:13-14 speaks of the church is a community founded in Christ and marked with a seal—the presence of the Spirit—that is a foretaste of the reign of Christ that is yet to come. The seal of the Spirit is the gift that serves as the pledge of God's love, presence and power in the church. This same image and reference—the seal that is a foretaste of the day of redemption—comes up again in Ephesians 4:30. This seal of the Spirit establishes the church as the dwelling place of God or temple of the Spirit, built together "in the Spirit" (Ephesians 2:22). Thus in Ephesians we have a trinitarian appreciation for what it means to be the church: the church is the *people* of God, the *body* of Christ, and the *fellowship* of the Spirit.

Thus, working primarily from but not exclusively from the book of Ephesians, what follows is a reflection on the church in its *local* expression: the gathered people of God in this time and in this place, in this neighborhood and city. Then, in the next chapter, I will consider what it means to speak of the church in its global engagement and witness. The two are distinct but inseparable. The church local is always part of the global Christian community, and the church global is ultimately about the gathering week in and week out of this community, as *this* local expression of the body of Christ, who gather "in the Spirit." We begin there: the church local.

THE UNITY OF THE CHURCH

First, we must speak of the unity of the local church. The church is only "holy, catholic and apostolic" if the church is "one." Everything about the church depends on a shared common life. Ephesians speaks to this against the backdrop of the notable distinction that was made between Jew and Gentile who, we read, are now one people of God (Ephesians 3:5-6) who, as the text stresses, "both . . . have access in one Spirit to the Father" (Ephesians 2:18).

This finds tangible expression within a local community of faith. We must speak of ecumenism and the calling of the Spirit to maintain the unity of the church—which I will do in the next chapter—but our reflections need to begin with the local church. We cannot be ecumenical until we learn what it means to maintain a living embodiment of this unity, this common identity as the body of Christ, within this local expression of the church.

It is noteworthy, of course, that the unity of the church is given and sustained, created, by the Spirit. It is the fruit of the Spirit's presence and power within the local assembly of the people of God. And its genius is that there is unity with diversity—Jew and Gentile highlighted in Ephesians. The unity of the church is not a human construct. It is not a unity of homogeneity of social class or race or ethnicity or even political affiliation, such as when a congregation is made up of the same demographic, where one is worshiping with those who share basic sensibilities and so unity comes more easily. Rather, the unity of the church should be a source of surprise and amazement, as a diverse group reflects a common faith and a shared life in the Spirit.

Similarly, the unity of the church is not one of control or compliance; it is not merely a single approach to governance that brings about unity. Thus while structures and leadership and authority "house" the unity, the unity is not created or fostered by church structure but by the witness and grace of the Spirit. Leadership is essential, but leadership is not ultimately what makes the church one. True unity cannot be fostered by a charismatic or autocratic leader, and it cannot be demanded as such.

Yes, we will likely be drawn to worship with those who are like-minded. And yes, structures of governance and decision-making are vital. But neither of these is the genius of what makes the church one. Rather, unity is the *fruit* of the work of the Spirit. Those in formal positions of power and influence can and must use their office to protect and defend the unity of the church, but never by demanding compliance. Rather, they insist on diversity and preserve unity, as Paul does when in Romans 14 he acknowledges major differences of opinion and conviction—matters of substance—within the congregation in Rome. But in the end, he does not insist on agreement or compliance; rather, he concludes the segment by insisting that they welcome one another in the Lord (Romans 15:7). The unity of the church is foundational to everything that it means to be the church, including teaching, preaching, mutual edification, the celebration of the Eucharist, worship, and governance.

This means that we cannot take conflict lightly. When it arises, as it inevitably will, we can appreciate that it might well foster new learning and strengthened relationships. But conflict can also be destructive and undercut the shared life of the church, grieve the Spirit, and compromise the mission of the church. Thus, the call to maintain the unity of the Spirit in the bond of peace needs to include the capacity to manage conflict and work toward resolutions that strengthen what it means to be the body of Christ. This work of conflict management and peacemaking is an essential spiritual gift—a profound way by which we tend to the work of the Spirit in our midst. This shared identity, this unity, cannot be taken for granted, so we *tend* it—we maintain the unity of the Spirit in the bond of peace—through mutual submission (Ephesians 5:21), kindness, and forgiveness

(Ephesians 4:30-31). We are eager to maintain the unity of the church, for we know that few things so grieve the Spirit as the church in disunity (Ephesians 4:30).

How do we maintain the unity of the Spirit? We get a hint of the response to this question when we come to the grand culmination—the "therefore" of the book of Ephesians. All that is said thus far leads the apostle to call the church to be filled with the Spirit, where he also speaks to those qualities or actions that mark this shared life:

> Do not get drunk with wine, for that is debauchery; but be filled with the Spirit, as you sing psalms and hymns and spiritual songs among yourselves, singing and making melody to the Lord in your hearts, giving thanks to God the Father at all times and for everything in the name of our Lord Jesus Christ. Be subject to one another out of reverence for Christ. (Ephesians 5:18-21)

Note that believers are filled with the Spirit as they sing songs, hymns, and spiritual songs, singing and making music in their hearts (v. 19). It is intriguing to see the close affinity between music and the filling of the Spirit. Is there a sense in which we are filled with the Spirit even as we sing together, that in our singing together we are lifting up our hearts to God so that we might be filled with the grace and power of God? And what must not be missed is that this shared life is marked by thanksgiving (v. 20); gratitude is a fundamental disposition that gives the church a capacity to live in the fullness of the Spirit. And then further, those in the faith community learn to live in mutual submission (v. 21), yet another vital way by which we maintain the unity of the Spirit in the bond of peace.[2]

---

[2]The NRSV unnecessarily inserts a subheading between Ephesians 5:20 and 21: "The Christian Household." What can easily be missed is that this call of verse 21 to mutual submission

Thus when we greet one another in the midst of our shared worship—the welcome of the other, or as in some circles, "the passing of the peace"—this act is done *in the Spirit*. As those who sing praise together and engage the Word together and move to the table together, we turn to the other, and our greeting signals that in the Spirit we welcome one another, we forgive one another, and we serve one another even if we differ strongly on a particular matter. All of this is done to maintain the unity of the Spirit in the bond of peace.

EDIFICATION: PREACHING, TEACHING, AND THE GIFTS OF THE SPIRIT

Then, second, we need to speak about edification. Yes, it is the work of the Spirit to bring unity, but this unity is not an end in itself. Unity is the soil in which fundamental work happens: God's people move from infancy to maturity, they grow together as each part does its work, a shared agenda is fueled and sustained by love (Ephesians 4:11-16). The ministry of the Spirit is anchored in the gifts given by Christ to the church—apostles, prophets, evangelists, pastors, and teachers, who equip one and all to contribute to the life and witness of the church so that all are maturing in the faith.

First and fundamentally, this growth in faith toward maturity is fueled and sustained by preaching and teaching. These are the offices that are given by Christ so that the church is equipped for every good work. These teaching offices naturally play a privileged role in the church, whether it is the proclamation of the word in

---

may well apply to the home, but it just as surely applies to the church community. We must not miss, within the church, this call to mutual deference to one another. This is evident week in and week out in every aspect of the church, but perhaps as significant as anything in the resolve to sing together, with one voice, the hymns and spiritual songs of the faith.

the context of shared worship, or in the complementary ministry of teaching that accompanies the preached word.

All this preaching and teaching is oriented to the Scriptures, of course, but with intentional dependence on the Spirit to illumine minds, rekindle hearts, and strengthen the will. As in chapter 6, it needs to be stressed that all preaching should be anticipated by the invocation of the Spirit as the essential act that precedes and prepares hearts and minds to hear the Word. The Word is not effective alone.

The ministerial office, the gifts or offices for which one from within the church might be ordained, should not be equated with the church (the church is the people of God, not the clergy alone). Those ordained to these offices are placed within God's people. The office is exercised as part of the integral life of the community of faith, and the ability of those in ordained ministry to be a means of grace to the community is dependent on their conscious and deliberate appropriation of the witness and anointing of the Spirit.

Second, while the gifts of apostle, prophet, evangelist, and pastor-teacher are given by Christ to the church, Ephesians expands on this and speaks more broadly to "each part": "But speaking the truth in love, we must grow up in every way into him who is the head, into Christ, from whom the whole body, joined and knit together by every ligament with which it is equipped, as each part is working properly, promotes the body's growth in building itself up in love" (Ephesians 4:15-16). This reference to the contribution of "each part" leads us naturally to a consideration of an important theme in Scripture: that the Spirit anoints and equips and gifts the church, and that these gifts, these "charisms," are given so that the work of God in the church might be fulfilled. This suggests that the Spirit works not only in close tandem with the Word, as already noted, but also in close affinity and coordination with the members of the body who exercise these gifts given by the Spirit.

Much is made about the "gifts of the Spirit," and whole programs have been designed to help Christian believers identify their particular gifting. While there may well be some profit in this exercise, consider that the gifts of the Spirit as described, for example, in 1 Corinthians 12–14, are not so much given to individuals to exercise but rather to the church as a whole—so that the body of Christ is built up. Perhaps we can then conclude that all the charisms needed for the growth and maturity of the church are given to each congregation, and now it is not so much that we would each discern our gift as that we would live in these giftings by doing our part, within the church, to encourage our shared life. That is, we might move from one city to another and join a new faith community. Rather than announcing in our new church that "this is my gift of the Spirit," why not ask, "What is needed in this church, and in what ways might I serve? What charism of the Spirit might I exercise for the sake of *this* community?" While in your previous church you were active in teaching, perhaps you have come to a church with plenty of teachers, and so you might ask what is needed. This assumes some basic capacity or competency, of course, but the premise is that we ask what is needed and where we can best be of service.

We might consider the list of gifts in 1 Corinthians 12, and we can conclude that these were the gifts of the Spirit given to that congregation as those gifts that were needed in *that* context. The gifts are congregation-specific, reflecting how the Spirit is sustaining *that* church and fostering its capacity to flourish. Thus Gordon Fee, in reflecting on 1 Corinthians 12:8-10, speaks of these "manifestations" as diverse ways in which the Spirit is apparent in the gathered community. This list is, as Fee puts it, "tailored to the situation in Corinth."[3] This is a reminder that the gifts of the Spirit are not our personal possession, as in "I have the gift of discernment." Rather, we say that in this context we exercise this gift for the well-being and edification of this community.

Third, what of those more overt or seemingly visible manifestations of the Spirit? I am thinking here of the list in 1 Corinthians 12, notably healings, prophesying, discernment of spirits, and tongue-speaking. As most readers would know, there are two different perspectives in the contemporary church in this regard. Some teach that those gifts were only for an infant church, and over the centuries as the church has matured these gifts were left by the way. This perspective is typically spoken of as "cessationist." In contrast, there are those for whom these gifts are the primary if not the *definitive* evidence of the Spirit's presence, and thus these gifts are to be eagerly sought, in that they are the highest expression of the Spirit in the church.

Is there a third way? Can we affirm the gifts of the Spirit—including these manifestations—but locate them in ordered worship and ministry? Can we affirm that these more "spectacular" manifestations, for lack of a better word, have their place but can easily distract from Christ and from the deep and regular and graduated work of the Spirit? They are gifts of the Spirit, and yet they are to be exercised quietly and without drawing undue attention to the person who is exercising the gift. The distraction these gifts cause can undermine the ultimate agenda: maturity in Christ. The gifts of tongue-speaking with interpretation, or the gifts

---

[3]Gordon D. Fee, *Paul, the Spirit and the People of God* (Peabody, MA: Hendrickson, 1996), 154.

of healing and prophecy, can be a valuable contribution to the life of the community. However, they must be exercised with discretion and humility. Furthermore, the apostle Paul stresses that all exercise of gifts is for fostering maturity in Christ. We are to put away childish things (1 Corinthians 13:11), and in speaking specifically about the gifts he writes: "Brothers and sisters, do not be children in your thinking; rather, be infants in evil, but in thinking be adults" (1 Corinthians 14:20). He urges further that "all things should be done decently and in order" (1 Corinthians 14:40). The bottom line for the apostle is that we are growing and maturing toward what it means to be adults in our thinking and in our faith. Thus nothing must be done that distracts or undercuts the foundational gifts of teaching and preaching.

By speaking of the priority of teaching and preaching and the need for order and decency and maturity, I am suggesting that the life and witness of the church is sustained by the immediate presence and power of the Spirit. Clark Pinnock aptly notes: "The Spirit who filled Jesus empowers the community of disciples to be the vehicle of God's saving activity. . . . Like Jesus, the church must live not out of its own resources but by the power of the indwelling Spirit, which breathes, strengthens, inspires and guides."[4] That is the key: to live not a self-constructed life or a self-constructed church, but to live in community with a deep sense that this is the work of the Spirit. In unity, the unity of the Spirit that is exercised in love and hospitality for one another, we learn to speak the truth in love (Ephesians 4:15) as each one contributes as the means by which the Spirit works in the shared life of the church.

---

[4]Clark H. Pinnock, *Flame of Love: A Theology of the Holy Spirit* (Downers Grove, IL: InterVarsity Press, 1996), 115.

THE CHURCH IN WORSHIP: THE SPIRT,
THE ELEMENTS OF WORSHIP, AND THE ARTS

Every aspect of the life and witness of the church is animated by the Spirit. Nowhere is this truer and more critical than in worship, the simple but powerful act of common prayer. This is evident, at the least, in three aspects of worship.

First, in song. As already noted, we are called to sing psalms, hymns, and spiritual songs with gratitude, and do so in the fullness of the Spirit (Ephesians 5:18-20). Music is an essential capacity by which the church lives in the Spirit. We lift up our hearts by raising our voices in song, and the genius is that our worship is whole-hearted. We sing with abandon—not that it is loud, necessarily, but that it is authentic to the interior movement of our hearts.

Second, we move to the Word. As stressed already, the ministry of the Word—the text opened, read, proclaimed, and heard—is all done in the fullness of the Spirit.

And third, we move to the table in the full realization that the Eucharist, the Lord's Supper, is a gathering where the animating agent of the meal is the Holy Spirit. This meal is a means by which the people of God *remember* (looking back), *anticipate* (looking forward), and *encounter* the risen Christ in real time. Past, future, and present. All of this is a human act, of course. *We* remember; *we* anticipate; *we* meet Christ. And yet in this holy meal the primary actor is God. This is why the epiclesis is so important. Epiclesis is the ancient term that references the invocation for the active presence of the Spirit in the sacred meal. It is the prayer, or some variation of the prayer, "Come, Holy Spirit, come and take these simple things, bread and cup, and sanctify them so that they are to us the body and blood of Christ; and come and sanctify us, those who come to the table, that we might participate in a manner that reflects your call on our lives." Here we have something to learn from the Eastern church. Alexander Schmemann makes this point, from this tradition but as a word to all Christians, when he writes: "It is the Holy Spirit who manifests the bread as the body and the wine as the blood of Christ. The Orthodox Church has always insisted that the *transformation* (*metabolē*) of the eucharistic elements is performed by the *epiclesis*—the invocation of the Holy Spirit—and not by the words of institution."[5]

Listen for the epiclesis—the prayer within the words of invitation and institution, the invocation to the Father that in Christ the Spirit would come. When it is not there, it should jar us; we should feel that something is missing and at the least compensate for this in our own personal prayer as we come to the table.

Some have spoken of convergence worship—worship that is thoroughly Pentecostal and charismatic, with the first movement of worship marked by extended and ecstatic song that then moves to worship that is evangelical, with the reading and proclamation of Scripture to, then the third movement, the table—the sacramental. This may be a good and appropriate structure for contemporary worship. But the main point is that however we design worship—using contemporary or ancient liturgical models—all must be done by and in intentional dependence on the Spirit. This needs to be made explicit: we enter into the worship of the triune God, with our focus on Christ Jesus, the author and finisher of our faith, and do so by calling for the Holy Spirit to animate our song, illumine our minds as we engage the Scriptures, and sanctify to us the bread and the cup.

As an aside, we should not assume that louder music or a more emotionally intense service somehow signals a greater level of

---

[5] Alexander Schmemann, *For the Life of the World: Sacraments and Orthodoxy* (Crestwood, NY: St. Vladimir's Seminary Press, 1998), 43-44. Emphasis Schmemann's.

Spirit-presence. The Spirit is certainly present in the ecstatic praise and adoration of the people of God—the hearty amen and hallelujah! But we also need to note that the Spirit is often known through the deep silence that interspaces our worship. We do not need to fear silence. Rather, even if we are uncomfortable with it, we can appreciate that the Spirit is just as often present in the silence, the stillness, and the spaces between the various elements of our worship. We can move from song to Scripture in silence. We can give space for silence in the prayers of confession or after the reading of Scripture or as we move together to the Lord's Table. Silence is an important feature of true Christian worship, and the point here is that silence is indispensable to cultivating an awareness of the Spirit's presence in our worship.

Finally, in speaking of Spirit-inspired and empowered worship, we need to link these comments back to what was highlighted in chapter 3 regarding the Spirit and creation and then the Spirit and the arts, where reference was made to Bezalel and his colleague Oholiab. When we speak of the Spirit and Christian worship, we must recognize the essential role of the arts in worship—from architecture, to design, to music, dance, the dramatic, and the visual arts. As noted, Bezalel was filled with the divine Spirit (Exodus 31). He was given "ability, intelligence and knowledge" so that "artistic designs" support worship and liturgical leadership. It follows that Christian worship would draw on their contributions.

If beauty through the arts is essential to the presence and power of the Spirit in the life and worship of the church, then we need to call for excellence in the cultivation and use of the skills of the Bezalels and Oholiabs within our congregations: in music, in architecture and design, in the visual and dramatic arts, and in dance. We reject banality and kitsch. We affirm the power of light to infuse our worship spaces with a sense of the creative power of God. We call the artists in our midst to bring their gifts into our worship because beauty matters and because their gifts are indispensable to our capacity to worship in the Spirit.

We celebrate their work, but of course we reject the cult of the celebrity. When the artists in our midst—musicians, visual artists and actors, dancers, and designers—offer their gifts, it is not all about them. For all artists, but especially for musicians and dancers, we must keep in mind that they are not the focus of our worship; they are not entertainers. Their self-presentation should downplay their own experience and involvement and intentionally draw attention to the one who is alone to be worshiped. The standing ovation might be fine in the context of the concert, but in worship our focus is not on the artist, even if quietly and insistently we thank them for their work and for their contribution to worship. They are there to aid, accompany, and encourage worship, not become the focus of our attention.

THE SPIRIT AND GOVERNANCE: THE LEADERSHIP OF CHRIST, DISCERNMENT, AND DECISION-MAKING

When we think about the life and mission of the church, we think about edification and worship, of course. But now we come to a theme that is increasingly front and center for Christian communities: governance. We need to consider the implications of our pneumatology for questions of administration, leadership, and decision-making—to ask what it means for the church to be led by Christ through the gracious work of the Spirit. This is a complex question, and while this is not more important than either edification or worship, it will take a little more time and space to consider what we mean when we speak about the role and place of the Spirit in the oversight of a congregation.

In approaching matters of governance and leadership, we first need to affirm a fundamental theological conviction: that Christ Jesus is the Lord of the church. Christ is the leader; he is the one to whom all authority in heaven and earth has been given (Matthew 28:18). What we long for is the benevolent leadership of Christ; his authority is life-giving and transformative. Thus authority is not ceded to a human actor—pastor or priest or deacon or elder. It is not that Christ has left and now others are "in charge," but rather that Christ, in real time, actually exercises his brilliant and benevolent authority in the church. The point, of course, is that this authority of Christ is exercised through the immediate presence of the Spirit in the life, work, and witness of the congregation.

But how? There are two essential elements of that leadership and authority. First, Christ has established a structure or form of leadership: elders and priests and pastors and preachers. Those in these offices have real authority; they are stewards of the church and, as we read in 1 Peter, the people of God are called on to defer to this leadership. These offices are linked to the ascended authority of Christ (see Ephesians 4:11). However, this leadership is not absolute; there is not a one-to-one correlation between what those in leadership roles say and what Christ says, what they do and what Christ is doing. Yes, they have real authority, and when they speak—when they preach from the pulpit, for example—they speak the Word of Christ with authority. But it is a conditional and *contingent* authority. It is not final; it is not absolute; they are not little Christs. And yet, with this essential qualifier, when they humbly serve and come to their roles with an appreciation of this contingency, they are the gift of Christ to the church. We need them; we need good governance. We need leadership, and we recognize this through the formal laying on of hands and the anointing oil of consecration (2 Timothy 1:6-7). The Spirit's anointing is given to those in formal leadership roles within the structure and governance of the church.

But we can also speak of the *immediacy* of the Spirit's guidance for the church. It is surely not the case that Christ appoints and the Spirit anoints, and then those who have been placed in leadership are now "in charge" without further reference to Christ and the Spirit. Rather, could it also be that Christ's leadership and ministry—through the guidance of the Spirit—is *not* limited to the structures and offices and formal processes and protocols of good governance? Can we speak of an unmediated witness of the Spirit to the community? Can we speak not only of individual discernment but of *communal* discernment that complements the formal structures of offices, governances, and leadership?

In the book of Acts, we seem to see the potential for both functioning in tandem: both the formal structures that are essential to good governance and order—including the contingent but genuine authority of those in positions of leadership—as well as the unmediated witness of the Spirit to the whole community. If so, it may be that the best approach to decision-making and leadership includes the capacity to tend the formal systems of governance—who reports to who, who has the authority to speak, act, and make decisions that affect the church—but also, while tending these systems, have mechanisms in place by which we ask, What is the Spirit saying to us at this time and in this place?

In an earlier book on the theme of discernment, I addressed principally the question of individual discernment and then provided some preliminary thoughts on communal discernment.[6] There I referenced observations from Inagrace Dietterich that in effect dismissed both the structure of the church and the input from one and all. She writes, "Discerning communities are not hierarchical in structure, but neither are they egalitarian. . . . The focus . . . is not on the prerogatives of the designated leaders or on the equal privileges of the members, but on the corporate responsibility for discerning the wisdom and prompting of the Holy Spirit."[7] Thus, in her mind, discerning communities "are neither autocratic . . . nor democratic . . . but pneumocratic."[8]

When I first read Dietterich, her dismissal made sense to me. But now I wonder if this is a false polarity. Why must we pit these against one another? Why can we not view the formal offices of the church as a gift from Christ and a means by which the Spirit guides the church? Why speak of "pneumocratic" as an approach that is over against hierarchical? Why dismiss the structure and, as she seems to do, suggest that if it is leader-led it is autocratic? Why not affirm the indispensable role of James, as the head of the church in Jerusalem, to the process of discernment described in Acts 15? And then also, why not view "democratic" as not so much that every voice has equal vote as rather that each does have something they can contribute? Sure, some will have a particular gift and wisdom and powers of observation that they will bring to the process. We will lean into those who may bring particular expertise.

---

[6]Gordon T. Smith, *The Voice of Jesus: Discernment, Prayer and the Witness of the Spirit* (Downers Grove, IL: InterVarsity Press, 2003).

[7]Darrell L. Guder et al., *Missional Church: A Vision for the Sending of the Church in North America* (Grand Rapids, MI: Eerdmans, 1998), 173-74. This was a team-written book but Deitterich was the lead writer for this chapter.

[8]Guder et al., *Missional Church*, 174.

Perhaps an intentional approach to communal discernment leverages rather than dismisses the dynamic and iterative interplay between the formal offices and leadership roles of the church and the wisdom and perspective of the assembly as a whole. We may work with both the structures that are essential to good governance but also a process of listening and being attentive, where we suspend the rules and the structures so that we can intentionally attend to the witness and guidance of the Spirit from those who are not in formal positions of authority. It is not that we are denying the importance of formal structures. It is merely that we are suspending them, one might say, in order to ask the whole community: What is the Spirit saying to us?

In our normal structures of governance, we naturally privilege those voices in positions of power and influence. But when the structures are suspended for an exercise in discernment, it might well mean that we attend to different voices or perspectives, reflecting the diverse ways in which different members of the congregation see and experience how the church is fulfilling its identity and its mission. And so we listen to these voices.

First, there is the voice of *experience*. The Wesleyan theological and spiritual tradition has always recognized the primacy of Scripture in theological formulation and the importance of tradition, but it has also seen that our theological vision must be informed by experience. We have to ask, What is the Spirit saying to us through our experience of what God is doing in our midst and in our world? In the book of Acts, this was clearly a huge variable in the movement of the early church in coming to terms with the spiritual journey and experience of the emerging Gentile Christian community. Thus, for example, Peter unapologetically appealed to experience when he defended his actions in baptizing

Cornelius and his household. He was criticized for going to and eating with the uncircumcised (Acts 11), but then Peter told the story of why he went to the home of Cornelius and what happened, and by so doing he silenced his critics. He appealed to *experience* to highlight something that the Spirit was signaling to the church. I am suggesting that we might also ask what it means to attend to the experience of the Christian community when seeking to discern what God is saying to the church today.

Second, we attend to the Spirit by learning to listen to those at the margins—those who are not in positions of power and influence. Often we default in our listening to those with power and influence; we can so easily, it would seem, give them a privileged voice at the table. But could it be that some of the most significant things that the Spirit is wanting to say to the church is coming from those who are at the margins—with neither influence or power—and that it therefore behooves us to find ways to hear them and attend to their voice? I think of the remarkable work of Robert Ekblad, for example, and the genius of his publication that says so much with the title: *Reading the Bible with the Damned.*[9] His contention is that we need to learn what it means to read the Bible with those who are in prison, or those who are displaced or refugees, or those who feel that their lives do not count for much or for anything.

Third, we attend to the Spirit when we listen to those who are at the front lines of service for and with the church: those who are actually doing what we are called to do. For example, it means that as the president of a university I listen to the faculty—those who are in the classroom and actually doing the teaching and engaging the students in the mission of the university. Denominational leaders

---

[9]Robert Ekblad, *Reading the Bible with the Damned* (Louisville, KY: Westminster John Knox, 2005).

listen to those who give leadership to local churches—pastors and both clergy and lay parish leadership. It means that a nonprofit development agency listens to those who are in the field, doing the very work that the mission or the organization is committed to. I wonder what it might mean for a local church to listen to those who are serving on the front lines. Perhaps it is listening to the usher who notices that a certain demographic of the congregation always sit at the end of the pew, or those in youth ministry who are picking up signals as they spend time with young people and learn about both their hopes and aspirations and their fears and points of stress. Or we find a way to listen to the seniors in our midst and ask how and in what ways the Spirit may be present to us through their experience. In each case, we learn to listen not just twice as much but as the general tenor of our engagement with the other. We listen.

And then, when it comes to making decisions and speaking in the name of God, we find a way to integrate what we have heard the Spirit saying to us through these various voices or sources with the structures of governance and authority that have been put in place by Christ and anointed with Christ's Spirit. As noted, Acts 15 is a potential case study of this in the Scriptures—a remarkable and encouraging example of the early church that was discombobulated by the experience of Paul and Barnabas in the hinterland and their suggestion that Gentiles were fully Christian without first becoming Jews. They listened to one another and especially to Paul, and in the end it was James, the formal leader of the church, who declared that it seemed good to them and to the Holy Spirit that Gentiles are fully Christian without having to first become Jewish (Acts 15:28). James legitimized that process.

I am proposing an intentional process of listening, learning, and discerning that affirms and leverages both the formal structure and governance of the church and the moderated but open and attentive approach of active listening to these diverse voices that are often a means by which the Spirit is speaking to and guiding the church. This dynamic might provide a congregation or even a denomination with a way of making sense of the witness of God's Spirit for some vexing and challenging questions—whether it is matters of liturgy and worship, matters of missional strategy, or questions of ethics and moral integrity.

In all of this, the role of the moderator is crucial. The genius of Acts 15 is not merely that they discerned well together but that they had someone in place who had the authority and gifting to preside over and in the conversation, leading them to say: "It seems good to the Holy Spirit and to us that . . ." This capacity to moderate the conversation is surely one of the most urgently needed gifts for the church in our day, when the church is so easily polarized around a whole range of issues and when it seems that we only know how to enter into a process that is marked by winner-take-all. In such a setting, the moderator—who brings not unanimity, necessarily, or even consensus, but rather a shared vision of the way forward even when there is a minority voice—is so crucial. It requires a special posture of detachment and holy indifference, and, most of all, attentiveness to the movement of the Spirit in the community.

In the end, Christ is the Lord of the church, and it is the Spirit whose witness must be given primacy. Human appointments and offices matter. The church needs women and men who will accept the call of God and the anointing of the Spirit and serve in leadership roles—as pastors and priests, as elders and deacons—and provide the due diligence of working on committees and participating in the governance of the church. We must thank those who serve in this capacity, whether clergy or lay, whether employed with a modest salary or serving as volunteers. But these roles of authority and responsibility only work if we hold them lightly—that is, if we carry them with diligence and then let them go when it is time for another to pick up the baton.

The danger is that so frequently the charismatic leader or the long-serving leader comes to assume that they have *inherent* authority by virtue of their office or their experience of the Spirit or their capacity to testify to how the Spirit has "anointed" them. The longer such a person is in the role, the more difficult it can be to challenge their authority; they no longer serve with genuine accountability; they so easily assume that their word is God's word. It does make one wonder whether there is a shelf life to leadership in the church, or whether at the least we need to ask God to spare us from those who assume that the longer they are in the office the more they are "institutionalized" within their role—as senior pastor, or chair of the church council, or whatever role it might be that now has become so overly associated with one person that it is difficult for us to truly attend to the fresh winds of the Spirit.

CONCLUSION

The church is sustained by the gracious work of the Holy Spirit. And so we should pray that the Spirit would come and make us one, gift us and anoint us so that we might become mature in Christ, direct and empower our worship and guide our church to be all that we are called to be. This is a call for intentionality—that we find the ways and means by which we can consciously lean into the grace of the Spirit in worship, education, and governance. That is, in all aspects of what it means to be the church, we welcome the Holy Spirit with open and eager hearts and minds.

CHAPTER EIGHT

THE SPIRIT AND
THE CHURCH GLOBAL

C HRIST CALLS THE CHURCH to participate in the mission of God—whether it is the calling to witness to the reign of Christ from Jerusalem to Judea to the ends of the earth ("You are my witnesses," Acts 1:8) or the call to disciple the nations ("Go therefore," Matthew 28:19), or the example of the early church that embraced this invitation to be part of the purposes of God in the world. This chapter will consider how this engagement with the mission of God is specifically in and by the Spirit. The Spirit calls, equips, empowers, and then guides the church to be part of the mission of God in the world.

It is important to stress that the purposes of God in the world are not limited to the speaking or the actions of the church. We speak of an *ecclesial* pneumatology, but we do so knowing full well that the presence and work of the Spirit is not limited to the confines of the church. Yet we can still ask, What is the connection between the Holy Spirit and the mission of God for the church? We seek a pneumatology that explains and informs how the church functions in its engagement with the world.

The Interplay of Divine and Human Agency

The church is called to participate in the mission of God, to witness in word and deed to the reign of God in the church and in the world. This work, this witness, while it is without doubt a *human* act, can only be thought of as human agency *empowered* and *guided* by the Spirit. Luke 24:49 speaks of the promise of the Father; the disciples are to wait in the city until they were "clothed with power from on high"—the power that Acts 1:8 specifically links to the Holy Spirit who will come upon them. Jesus is speaking of Pentecost, which would come ten days later. In the meantime, they were to wait. The mission of the church is necessarily a human endeavor that is guided and overseen and empowered by the Spirit.

It is important to highlight both that human agency matters and that it is human engagement in the grace and power of the Spirit. Consider Acts 13:1-4 as an example of the interplay between human agency and the ministry of the Spirit:

> Now in the church at Antioch there were prophets and teachers: Barnabas, Simeon who was called Niger, Lucius of Cyrene, Manaen a member of the court of Herod the ruler, and Saul. While they were worshiping the Lord and fasting, the Holy Spirit said, "Set apart for me Barnabas and Saul for the work to which I have called them." Then after fasting and praying they laid their hands on them and sent them off. So, being sent out by the Holy Spirit, they went down to Seleucia; and from there they sailed to Cyprus.

Yes, the church in Antioch did what they were called to do. They discerned what the Spirit was saying and then "laid hands on them and sent them off." And yet, after reading that they "sent them off" (v. 3), in the next sentence we read that they were "sent out by the Holy Spirit" (v. 4).[1] Which is it? Was it the mission and the sending of the church in Antioch? Or was it the mission and sending of the Spirit? That is a false question, of course, because the answer to the question is "yes": it was the church in Antioch acting in response to and in tandem with the Spirit.

In other words, there is no reason to pit divine and human agency against each other as though the mission of God in the world is one-dimensional. It may sound more spiritual to insist that it is "all of the Spirit"—that when the Spirit works it is unilateral, with no human element muddying the waters, that some event or development was "the pure work of God" as a way of signaling that something seemingly had no human actor.

But while no doubt the Spirit does what only the Spirit can do, it is still important to affirm that the work of the Spirit consistently happens in and through the words and actions of human agents. Gabriel comes to Mary and invites her to accept the conception within her by the Spirit, and she must say the words: "May it be to me according to your word." She must do what *she* must do.

And it truly is both the church in Antioch that "sent them off" *and* that they were "sent out by the Holy Spirit." This is not a contradiction or an inconsistency. Human agency matters *not* because the church is filled with heroes and messiahs who accomplish great things for God but because God has chosen to work with human persons who speak and act in the name of Christ. And they are not mere puppets or robots. They are full participants in the redemptive purposes of God.

---

[1]Here is another example of where the NRSV inserts an unfortunate heading into the translation of the text. Between Acts 13:3 and Acts 13:4 is inserted the heading "The Apostles Preach in Cyprus," and the consequence is that we might miss how human and divine agency are twinned.

And yet the church is deeply dependent on the Spirit and, more specifically, it is the church on mission in an intentional *responsiveness* to the Spirit. The Spirit must take the lead; the church responds to that lead. Thus when we think about mission and the Spirit we must consider the crucial place of discernment. This means asking how and in what ways the Spirit is at work in *this* time and in *this* place. And how can our work, our engagement with the world in word and deed, more clearly reflect an alignment with what the Spirit is doing?

For example, I live and work in Canada and see the character of global mission from that vantage point. From this perspective, when we ask, "What on earth is the Spirit doing?," we see many movements or footprints of the Spirit. We see that the epicenter of global mission is shifting to the Global South—toward China, Korea, India, and the Southern Cone of Latin America. If the Iberian Peninsula was the epicenter of global mission in the seventeenth and eighteenth centuries, and the British Isles in the nineteenth century, and the United States and Canada in the twentieth century, then what does it mean for engaging in global mission from Canada and as the Canadian church if the epicenter of global mission has shifted yet again? It would seem to be the case is that if this is so, then the role of the Canadian church will also change: the Canadian church is still involved in global mission, but in a different way, with a new paradigm.

Then also we see the emergence of what is often spoken of as "marketplace ministries," with a growing number of business leaders called into mission through the work of business, the production and selling of products and services. The "business as mission" or "kingdom business" movement urgently needs to get beyond only viewing mission as a cover or mechanism for doing traditional mission; when this shift happens, it represents a new work of the Spirit who is calling women and men into the arts and education as well as business. That is, what is emerging is an awareness that those called into education, business, and the arts are colleagues and partners with those called into religious leadership to establish and lead faith communities and do the work of pioneer evangelism. They are front and center—not mere supporters of, but key participants in the work of the Spirit.

And then also, of course, Western Europe, the United States and Canada, Australia and New Zealand—all countries that in previous times were sending missionaries elsewhere—are now finding that the world has come to them. This also fundamentally changes the way in which the church in these countries engages the call to global mission. The changing paradigm for global mission means that rather than thinking of the world as "overseas," or that mission is by nature an international endeavor, now those of other religious persuasions are our neighbors.

And then, as big as anything, the world in which many of us live and work is increasingly secular. Yes, it is a pluralist society, but the most significant factor may be the marginalization of religion so that now the church is on mission in a secular age. Might it be the case that the emergence of a secular West is actually of the Spirit? Søren Kierkegaard would have assumed as much—the decline of Christendom was not, in his mind, a problem or a tragedy but rather the imperative of the Spirit for the sake of the church and the kingdom. Consequently, rather than hand-wringing and wondering what went wrong, why not actually see this as providential? Then we can ask and discern how it is that the Spirit is doing the work of God in this time and place.[2]

---

[2]This is essentially the point I make in Gordon T. Smith, *Wisdom from Babylon: Leadership for the Church in a Secular Age* (Downers Grove, IL: IVP Academic, 2020).

We then engage our world with courage and wisdom and discernment. We name a new reality and then respond by asking what is required of us now, in the situation that presents itself, not how we might wish it were.

The church of each region of the world needs to do this due diligence. The above provides one example of how the church in one part of the world might read the times and see them as evidence of the footprints of the Spirit. Surely we need to think on a global and national scale, but we should also do the same exercise as a local church within a neighborhood or city. We should ask, "What is the Spirit doing and calling us to do?" Rather than "franchising"—heading off to a church conference to learn the most recent method for church growth and mission—we can ask instead how we, as a church community, are being called to *this* town or city in response to the critical needs and opportunities that reflect the agenda of the Spirit in *this* location. This means that the church in my region of the world does not presume to tell the church in another region or continent or set of circumstances how the Spirit is guiding them. And it means that within a church we might be in conversation with churches in another part of town—learning from and with one another, and perhaps challenging one another. We respect the capacity of the other to discern how God is calling them to be present to their city or neighborhood.

Perhaps we should think in terms of concentric circles. Consider your immediate neighborhood. What is the Spirit up to, and how is the Spirit calling your congregation in your immediate context and setting? Think of your city or region or country and ask, How and in what ways is the Spirit calling the church to be present to this social, cultural, and economic system? How is the church in Lebanon uniquely called to be present to Lebanon or the church in the Philippines present to their country? And then, finally, what do we see happening on the global scene, and what might it mean for what the Spirit is calling us to be here, in this place, so that while we are local we are the church with a global vision of the work of the Spirit?

We must remember that the Spirit is seemingly in no hurry. We can let the Spirit do the Spirit's work in the Spirit's time, and in the meantime ask where we are invited to plant or water or harvest. We do not need to be heroes; we do our work confident that the purposes of the Spirit will happen as the Spirit brings to fulfillment the purposes of God—in the perfect timing of the Spirit.

MISSION AND CULTURE: MISSION AND "THE RELIGIONS"

When we think about mission and pneumatology, it is not long before we have to ask how we think about the question of the religious and cultural contexts in which the faith is being established, and how we can see questions of religion and culture through the lens of the presence and power of the Holy Spirit. No sector of the global Christian community has pressed this point so thoroughly as that of the Christian East—particularly theologians from China, India, and Korea. Their work might have significant implications for those who minister in the secular West in terms of how we respond to secularism—an ideology that is quasi-religious in character.[3]

As we enter into this reflection on the mission of the church and the encounter with other religious systems, we begin with a key

---

[3]In much of what follows, I am particularly indebted to Kirsteen Kim, *The Holy Spirit in the World: A Global Conversation* (Maryknoll, NY: Orbis, 2007). This is an excellent and essential resource that brings together mission theology and the theology of the Spirit.

affirmation: that the work of the Spirit is not confined to the visible boundaries of the church or to those who represent the church in mission. The work of the Spirit is not the same as the work of those who represent or are sent by the church, and the work of the Spirit is not limited by but actually both precedes and anticipates the work of those who act on behalf of the church. The Spirit cannot be controlled or domesticated by the church. The church is wise when it fosters a capacity to discern the presence of the Spirit that has often preceded and anticipated Christian witness.[4]

The work of the Spirit consistently pushes boundaries, fostering new, creative perspectives and approaches. As feminist and womanist theologians have insisted, the mission of the church is one of discerning and aligning heart and soul and mind with the work of the Spirit. We do not control, but groan with the Spirit and attend as a mother in childbirth to the birth-pangs of the world and the cosmos. And more, we affirm that the Spirit's work goes before the church and is active in contexts and settings long before the church is aware, potentially, of these developments. As significant as anything coming out of Vatican II was this revolutionary realization: that the Spirit of God was at work in other contexts and settings besides the Church of Rome. This opened the door to ecumenism, but also to an appreciation of the need for interfaith conversations and learning.

Then also, when we think about pneumatology and mission, we see that the Spirit's ministry will be different in each *cultural* context. Canadian Lutherans will worship and witness in a different way from Indonesian Lutherans—let alone Indonesian

---

[4]This perspective is ably articulated by Oscar García-Johnson in his *Spirit Outside the Gate: Decolonial Pneumatologies of the American Global South* (Downers Grove, IL: IVP Academic, 2019).

Pentecostals. Cultural motifs and emphasis, cultural patterns of life and work, including language and ways of thinking, will inform the way that the gospel is contextualized among each people group. The gospel and the church are not transplanted—if by that we mean that the identical tree is now located in new soil. Well, it is transplanted, but now this soil fundamentally alters the fruit from the tree. Thus a wine varietal has a different aroma and taste from region to region, which is why wine connoisseurs speak of the terroir—the soil and the way the soil transmits a distinctive flavor.[5] In like manner, the gospel is enculturated in *particular* soil—this social, cultural situation.

This means that if we are attentive to the presence and power of the Spirit we must learn to read the Scripture text and the Christian intellectual and spiritual tradition through the lens of those who come from a different social, cultural, and economic situation. There will always be both continuity and discontinuity when the Spirit locates the church within a cultural context—including sensibilities, beliefs, and practices—such that we must ask: Can we speak of the Spirit "sanctifying" the cultural and religious rites and expressions of those who receive the gospel—in their own time and place?

The tension here in conversations and debates about gospel and culture is whether it is appropriate to speak of not just a transcendent Spirit, who is over all things, but also an "immanent Spirit" who is in the world and whose presence is often felt through the "spirit"

---

[5]Learning from the gardener and the wine maker is a good way to think about how the gospel is enculturated. Thus Terry Theise insists, "When wine is at home, it settles in and starts to transmit. . . . We 'hear' those transmissions in flavors," and the wine "sends clear message of the soil, a panoply of nuances of fruits, flower and stones, flavors that are consistent, specific, and repeated year after year, varied only by the weather in which that year's grapes ripened." *Reading Between the Wines* (Berkeley: University of California Press, 2010), 75.

theologies of other religious movements. In the first, the Spirit is other—and the work of the Spirit is discerned and recognized and affirmed by reference to Christ, the Scriptures, and the church. In the second, the Spirit is all around us and discovered or discerned in the social, cultural, and religious spheres in which we live.

There will be discontinuity; the gospel will always challenge every culture and social system. The Spirit will always "prove the world wrong about sin and righteousness and judgment" (John 16:8-10). The Spirit will always press against that which is antithetical to the gospel. But might there also always be continuity, not merely in the cultural artifacts—the outward forms that house the gospel—but also in the internal sensibilities, the awareness and understanding and expression of the spiritual? One example of this conversation that is current for the church in my context is how and in what ways the church in Canada is to encourage and affirm indigenous expressions of worship and piety that draw on both the forms but also the movements of the "spirit" that reflect ancient sensibilities and practice. This includes, for example, recognizing how the Christ story was prefigured in various ways by Sioux religious practices. But more, there is wisdom emerging from pre-settler indigenous perspectives that has continuing relevance for both indigenous and settler Christians in Canada—thinking here in particular of ancient practices.[6]

I can in this regard commend the Presbyterian Church of Canada, who at their General Assembly in 2013 outlined an extensive theological framework for engaging expressions of aboriginal spirituality including especially those that were typically of indigenous prairie belief systems: the pipe ceremony, the sun

---

[6]See the work of the late Richard Twiss, *Rescuing the Gospel from the Cowboys: A Native American Expression of the Jesus Way* (Downers Grove, IL: InterVarsity Press, 2015).

dance, the powwow, the sweat lodge, the medicine wheel, and the smudge ceremony. Each of these is ancient—practiced over hundreds of years. Each is viewed as integral to prairie indigenous identity. Each is a means by which they acknowledged the Creator God. We note these historically significant practices when we ask how the gospel must be incarnated within a culture or society. This means that we are attentive to ancient spiritual practices that now become the vehicles for the presence and ministry of the Holy Spirit: the drumming exercise; the practice of smudging prior to a gathering or as the opening act of a gathering that, in effect, calls for the Great Spirit, which we now see to be the Holy Spirit, to come and be among us and with us.

In like manner, Christians in Muslim, Hindu, and secular contexts might see points of discontinuity—where the Spirit is confronting and challenging "the gods of this age"—but also points of continuity that the Spirit is sanctifying practices and sensibilities as part of the way in which the Spirit is locating the gospel in this time and in this place. This, of course, means that the gospel lived out among Canadian indigenous communities will look different from the liturgy and worship of Euro-Canadian settler communities, even as the gospel will look different in a predominantly Hindu, Muslim, or secular context.

We must, of course, be radically christocentric and orthodox—intentionally trinitarian. But with this as our point of departure, we must be open and attentive and willing to be surprised and called into new learnings and new expressions of the Spirit's presence in our midst. This might suggest that we do not ask the "Christ, Scripture, orthodox?" question prematurely but first consider how the Spirit is at work *anticipating* Christ and the witness of Scripture, including how we might interpret Scripture.

Spiritual Conflict and the Need for Discernment

In all of this, we must further acknowledge that not all spirits or spiritual movements are benevolent. We speak not only of continuity, but also of discontinuity; this is a reminder that we must surely speak of a cosmic battle for the soul of the world.

On the one hand, though, we cannot unwittingly demonize something—call something evil that is actually good—simply because it is strange to our ears or sensibilities or merely makes us uncomfortable. There is nothing gained if we simply assume that if it is different or not overtly Christian, at least to our way of thinking, it is a malevolent spirit.

Yes, there is indeed a cosmic battle. But we must refuse any suggestion of a dualistic universe—that, somehow, we live and work in world of eternal good and evil. To the contrary, the ascended Lord is Lord of all; further, the Holy Spirit hovers over all, in much the same way as the Spirit hovered over the darkness and void referenced in Genesis 1:1.

Further, while we must affirm the reality of demonic forces that resist the work of the Holy Spirit, we should not equate resistance to the church with resistance to Christ. We need to be cautious in attributing evil to anything that seems to impede what it is that we think we are being called to do. We do not call good evil; but more, we also do not attribute evil—or at least a malevolent spirit—to anything that initially bothers us or makes us uncomfortable or even that causes us difficulty.

There are art forms—visual or dance forms, or forms of music—that may seem alien to our ear but are not for a moment evil or demonic. Further, we must resist any inclination to assume that the Spirit is somehow with us, that we have a special anointing and that therefore we have the inside track on authentic religion and spirituality. Yes, we do know something of the gospel, but we are the blind leading the blind. The forces of darkness run through our hearts and our social and family systems, and thus we cannot presume that we are light while the other is dark, that we somehow possess the gospel and bring it in a confrontational way to the other.

However, we must—in dialogue with those we serve and learn from—be open to identifying where there is an internal spiritual or an oppressive social structure that does need to be confronted. But we cannot do this with the other unless we are prepared to confront the idolatrous systems of our own cultural, religious, and social contexts.

All of this leads us to the complicated issue of discerning how the Spirit is taking the ancient text and illuminating the church in its theology and witness—not just in terms of the mission of God (as, for example, Acts 13:1-4) but also in terms of theology and ethics. The two are linked. The church in Jerusalem learned something fundamental about the purposes of God in redemption only when they saw things differently precisely *because* of the encounter with the Gentile world.

Theology and mission are linked. This is why we need to attend to what new learning emerges from the church in mission—from the engagement of the church with those at the margins. Thus Acts 15, the great learning of the Jerusalem church, only makes sense in light of the Spirit's call of the church in Antioch in Acts 13. The engagement with the Gentile world of Asia Minor was the catalyst for the church in Jerusalem to—in the Spirit—see things differently. Paul and Barnabas had seen this early on; they were the seers or prophets, but they made their case not merely on the basis of a reading of the text but by the experience they had of preaching the gospel to the Gentiles. And this brings us to the interplay of Scripture, tradition, and experience. When we ask what the Spirit is saying to the church and illuminating for the church from the Scriptures, our reading of the Scriptures will be informed by the *experience* of the church, particularly her experience in mission.

When the church reaches across cultures and ethnicities, the church will ask: What are we learning and experiencing that challenges our assumptions when we read the Bible? Thus, for example, the church in the West needs to learn from the church in the Global South. What perspectives emerge and considerations arise when we read the Bible alongside indigenous communities—for example, when settler New Zealanders read the Bible with the indigenous Maori, or when immigrants to Canada read the Bible alongside of the Inuit?

This means that we must be discerning. To discern is to recognize where and in what ways we can confidentially conclude that what we see, hear, or feel is genuinely of God. The work of discernment assumes that some things that might move us are actually not of God, and that some things that seem strange or different or uncomfortable are, actually, indicators of the presence and power of the Spirit. And this act of discernment informs each aspect of our engagement in the mission of God:

- What we say and choose not to say when we speak, but also when we choose to remain silent.

- What we do and choose not to do—recognizing that patience is a key indicator that we are letting the Spirit do the Spirit's work in the Spirit's time.

- What we affirm when it comes to new religious expressions and where we invest our energies when it comes to the essential work of ecumenism.

The work of discernment assumes a deep awareness of and attentiveness to the Scriptures. This essential caveat also assumes that we are always in a learning mode, always willing to see the ancient text through a new set of lenses, always reading the Scriptures with an open heart and mind. The Scriptures always remain foundational, yet the same Spirit who brought to us the Scriptures is now the Spirit who calls us to see and engage our current situation with wisdom and grace.

As the church, then, that lives by the dynamic of Word and Spirit, what might be the criteria by which we recognize and affirm the work of the Spirit in our midst? I offer the following three ways by which we might do this work of discernment: Christ Jesus as an essential referent, the fruit of the Spirit, and a commitment to care for the poor.

CHRIST JESUS AS OUR ESSENTIAL REFERENT

First, all discernment must begin with a radical orientation toward the person and glory of Christ. All discernment has Christ Jesus as its basic reference point. However, I must add two qualifiers. First, it is not just any Christ; it is the Christ who is the Son of the Father. It is the one by whom and through whom the Spirit is sent and, further, it is the Christ who bears human flesh and who is crucified and ascended to the right hand of the Father. We are not speaking of a spiritized Christ or a Christ who is the fruit of human projections but the Christ who is revealed in Scripture and testified to in the Nicene Creed.

But while it is vital to affirm that Christ is our referent, our compass, we recognize that we are all on a journey, a pilgrimage *toward* Christ. None of us have arrived; none of us have a special handle on Christ. Thus it is appropriate to consider what is fostering our desire to move toward Christ and to know Christ more and love Christ Jesus more deeply.

Being drawn to Christ will be evident, at least in part, in that we are freed from needing to be heroes—freed from feeling that we need to be the center of attention. We are willing to let others speak and let others lead. Denominationally, we are at peace when our collective work does not get affirmed or praised because we have chosen to work quietly and behind the scenes. Our ultimate desire is the glory of Christ, not our denomination or our church or our institutional brand. And throughout, we are attentive to how others are learning what it means to know the Jesus that is testified to for all of us through the Scriptures.

THE FRUIT OF THE SPIRIT

Then also we might ask about the *footprints* or traces of the Spirit in our circumstances—indicators that the Spirit is in our midst and drawing us to Christ and to the words and work to which we are called. We will be drawn to Christ, but more, we can also speak of the evidence—the fruit, the indicators—that something is of the Spirit. We will be called to greater generosity, kindness, and hospitality. We will build bridges rather than walls. We will be inclined toward compassion rather than anger or revenge or vindictiveness. We will err on the side of mercy rather than judgment. Consider the observation that Jesus makes in the Sermon on the Mount: that we are to beware of those who come as wolves in sheep's clothing. How do we recognize them? How do we discern if they are false prophets? His response: "You will know them by their fruits" (Matthew 7:16).

This does not mean for a moment that we are naive. It is rather that we choose a posture that is fundamentally benevolent and engage our work with a resilient joy that as much as anything opens our eyes to the signs of God's grace in the other and in our circumstances. When our hearts are filled with anger or fear, we are as often as not blind to the footprints of the Spirit, the indicators of the Spirit's presence, in the "other" and in our own circumstances. By resilient joy, I mean a joy in the midst of difficulty and suffering. As Paul himself puts it, it is a joy even in the midst of affliction, a consolation even in the face of difficulty (2 Corinthians 7:4).

Attentiveness to and Responsiveness to the Poor

When we think about the poor—the marginalized, the oppressed, the refugee, the homeless—it calls to mind the remarkable words of Jesus himself in the synagogue recorded in Luke 4. He makes a direct link between his personal anointing by the Spirit—that the Spirit is upon him—and his calling to bring good news to the poor. And then later, Jesus himself is insistent that we are only in tune with him when we feed the hungry, heal the sick, and clothe the naked (Matthew 25:35-40).

What are the ultimate criteria for authentic worship within the church? Whether it is truly and intentionally trinitarian and christocentric is surely a criterion. Whether the Scriptures are read and proclaimed is also essential, and if the proclaimed Word is accompanied by the table. But Isaiah 58 would suggest that worship is a sham if it is not marked by a parallel commitment to economic justice.

It is then perhaps no surprise that the early church was marked by a deep commitment to care for the poor and those in need (Acts 2:44-45) and to care for the widows in their midst (Acts 6:1-7). As intriguing as anything is the encounter referenced in Acts 15 that Paul had with the leaders of the church in Jerusalem. Paul sought to assure the elders in Jerusalem that indeed the Spirit was the one that was guiding his ministry and through him and his colleagues bringing Gentiles to faith in Christ. He receives the endorsement and affirmation of the Jerusalem elders. But it is interesting that when he speaks of this in the book of Galatians he adds this fascinating aside: "They [that is, the Jerusalem elders] asked only one thing: that we remember the poor, which was actually what I was eager to do" (Galatians 2:10). Some within the church will have this as their primary focus and ministry, but this is an important reference point for all of the ways in which the church is called to be engaged in the mission of God. If we are doing mission in the name of Christ and in response to the Spirit, it will be evident, in part, in this: "that we remember the poor."

There might well be other indicators or reference points for discernment. The Spirit, for example, will consistently challenge the "gods" of our age and of our culture. Thus we should also be attentive to the ways in which the Spirit is calling us to challenge the norms or assumptions of the prevailing culture of which we are a part. We might also speak of how the Spirit is not about monolithic sameness but rather that the sign of the Spirit in our midst is one of unity, but specifically a unity with diversity.

So yes, there might well be other criteria that might emerge for us in a conversation about effective discernment. The main point is that we must discern; we cannot be naive or assume that every impulse we have comes from God. Having said that, two more things need to be stressed. First, Kirsteen Kim rightly suggests that any one of our criteria (she works with a slightly different set) can happen alone and not truly be of God. Thus, she makes the helpful suggestion that the criteria or evidence of the Spirit must be "taken together."[7] We might have a remarkable commitment to social justice, but it is marked by an underlying tone of anger. We are on a zealous mission that propels us to do something that we are passionate about, and perhaps it is a good thing, but it is a way of engagement that has little to do with the person of Christ. Or we might be impressed that a person speaks about Jesus a great deal but with little or no evidence of a resilient joy or concern for the poor such that we wonder which "Christ" is being spoken about.

But second, as Kim notes, this work of discernment is not easy; it is complex and, further, it is "ongoing and provisional."[8] We are on a journey in our search for understanding and clarity of conviction. This means that discernment requires conversation, reflection, and accountability. Paul was deeply convinced that God was calling him and his colleagues to the Gentiles, but he was intentionally accountable to and in conversation with the elders in Jerusalem. The mission to the Gentles was complemented by this act of stepping back in reflection and discernment. The call of Acts 13 is matched by the visit to Jerusalem described in Acts 15 and in a subsequent visit by Paul to Jerusalem in Acts 21:17. Perhaps Paul's relationship with James provides us all with a model of intentional responsiveness to the Spirit that is complemented by a conversation and accountability with those who have a right and responsibility to be part of the conversation. So yes, we have

---

[7]Kirsteen Kim, *The Holy Spirit in the World: A Global Conversation* (Maryknoll, NY: Orbis, 2007), 169.
[8]Kim, *The Holy Spirit in the World*, 175.

criteria for discernment. I have suggested three. But our approach is always one that is, as Kim suggests, provisional: we test, with humility and with a disposition of continuous learning. And, further, we are accountable—not discerning in isolation but in community and conversation with our peers, including those of other cultural contexts and denominational traditions.

Mission and Ecumenism

The call to maintain the unity of the Spirit in the bond of peace (Ephesians 4:3) applies not only to the need for unity with diversity within the local church—a congregation—but it also has profound implications for the call to mission and global engagement and our relationship to Christians of other theological and denominational traditions that then, in turn, impacts our participation in the mission of God in the world. The prayer of John 17, "they may be one, as we are one," is linked directly to the call of the church to be in but not of the world. As soon as you bring pneumatology and mission together, you have to speak of the prompting of the Spirit that calls us to connect with women and men of other Christian theological and spiritual traditions. All the great twentieth-century missiologists were also ecumenists; they knew and recognized that schisms undermine and compromise the work of the Spirit to bring glory to Christ.

If we are attentive to the Spirit, we will find that the prompting of the Spirit will consistently foster within us a generosity toward Christians in other theological traditions. And yet it requires intentionality; it is so easy for us to default to our own tribes, the people we are most comfortable with, those with whom we tend to agree on theological and liturgical practice. We need to recognize the inner prompting of the Spirit that nudges us toward shared learning with and from those of other theological and liturgical traditions.

What this assumes is that no one church body is the gold standard—the unique bearer of the truth that has an edge on what it means to live in a manner that is both faithful to the Scriptures and the great tradition and uniquely knows the anointing of the Spirit. To the contrary, we humbly welcome the other and realize that we cannot attend to the new learning to which the Spirit is calling us unless we listen to the Christian through whom the Spirit is bringing light and wisdom not merely to their own tradition but for other Christians. We each bring our gifts—our spiritual insights—to the table, and learn from and with one another.

Thus we speak of unity *with* diversity. The solution is not a single church body—a monolithic institutional structure—but rather a unity that both recognizes and affirms the diverse theological and liturgical expressions of Christian faith and worship. In other words, we can actually celebrate our diversity and realize that in the providence of God, the Holy Spirit has housed particular wisdom within different traditions. Thus, for example, an evangelical might recognize that she needs Anglicans in her life so that she comes to a greater appreciation of the sacramental character of the grace of the Holy Spirit. And the Anglican might come to see the beauty of the work of the Spirit that comes to his attention through a friendship with someone of a Pentecostal background—who brings a vibrant appreciation of the immediacy of the Spirit's presence in life, work, and relationships.

Schism is never good. The break between the Eastern and Western Churches in the eleventh century was unfortunate, and the sixteenth-century Protestant Reformation, while perhaps in the minds of some a necessary breach, was no less tragic. And we can speak of other schisms in the nineteenth and twentieth centuries that surely grieved the Spirit. But perhaps now we see that the Spirit is working in and through these schisms to bring diversity of perspective. We cannot continue to grieve the Spirit and allow schism to be a source of continued conflict or division. We do not encourage schism, but when it happens, even if seemingly unavoidable, we then work to tend the unity of the church and find ways to be in Christian fellowship and shared ministry and learning with those of other Christian traditions.

Again, we come back to the central premise when we think about the Spirit and the church. We must be intentional in our engagement through mission with our context, with the other, with other religious communities. We must be attentive to how the Spirit is present in and through the other, and how the Spirit is nudging us to be more ecumenical in the ways in which we engage our local community, our country, and our world.

A CALL TO INTENTIONALITY

IS THERE A SINGLE OR ABIDING MESSAGE that lies at the heart of these reflections on the person and ministry of the Holy Spirit? If nothing else, all that has been offered here speaks to the need for *intentionality* and *attentiveness* with respect to our understanding and our experience of the person of the Holy Spirit and the grace that is known through the Spirit. It has been my prayer that this book would be a catalyst for both—for increased clarity of understanding, but then, of course, for greater capacity and responsiveness to the Spirit in our experience personally and in the life and witness of the church.

First, let's be attentive and intentional in our *understanding* of the person and ministry of the Spirit. Our approach to pneumatology and our conversation about the Holy Spirit can be thoughtful. This means that we are able to speak of the Spirit as one with the Father and the Son within the Trinity but also that with relative ease we can speak specifically to the four associations or relationships: the Spirit and Christ, the Spirit and creation, the Spirit and the Word, and the Spirit and the church. There are without doubt subsidiary questions—how we receive the gift of the Spirit and how we speak of the means of grace and how the Spirit interacts with culture or non-Christian religions. But if we have clarity on these four, we have the guideposts that can help us make our way through what often feels like a confusing maze. We can feel less hesitant to talk about the ministry of the Spirit with others, notably those of other theological and spiritual traditions.

And then, second, we move from understanding to *experience*. With openheartedness and receptivity, we welcome the Holy Spirit into our lives—individually and in the shared life of the church. We choose to live intentionally. We know what it is to ask for this extraordinary gift from the Father that is given to us in Christ so that we can walk in the Spirit and bear the fruit of the Spirit in our work and in our relationships. We can cultivate this intentionality and this attentiveness personally—aware of and responsive to the ways in which the Spirit is calling us into deeper fellowship with Christ and more generous engagement with Christ in the relationships to which we are called.

And as a faith community, as the church, we can be intentional and attentive to the ways in which we are being called and empowered by the Spirit—together in worship, governance, edification, and mission, to be today what it means to be the church that lives by and in the grace of the Spirit.

Few hymns capture this longing so remarkably as that of George Croly's "Spirit of God, Descend upon My Heart," published in 1854. Many of us come back to this hymn again and again when we say the prayer, "Come, Holy Spirit, come," and consciously choose to welcome the Spirit into our lives, our church, and our world:

Spirit of God, descend upon my heart;
Wean it from earth; through all its pulses move.
Stoop to my weakness, mighty as Thou art,
And make me love Thee as I ought to love.

Hast Thou not bid me love Thee, God and King?
All, all Thine own, soul, heart and strength and mind.
I see Thy cross; there teach my heart to cling:
Oh, let me seek Thee, and, oh, let me find!

Teach me to feel that Thou art always nigh;
Teach me the struggles of the soul to bear,
To check the rising doubt, the rebel sigh;
Teach me the patience of unanswered prayer.

Teach me to love Thee as Thine angels love,
One holy passion filling all my frame;
The kindling of the heav'n-descended Dove,
My heart an altar, and Thy love the flame.

To this end, we say: Welcome, Holy Spirit.

GENERAL INDEX

SCRIPTURE INDEX

ALSO BY GORDON T. SMITH

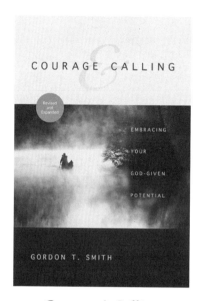

Courage & Calling
978-0-8308-3554-6

Teach Us to Pray
978-0-8308-4521-7

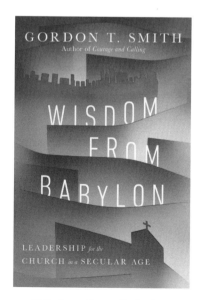

Wisdom from Babylon
978-0-8308-5326-7